MEMORIES OF
ROTHERHAM

The publishers would like to thank the following companies for their

support in the production of this book

ASD Lighting PLC

Ben Bennett JR Ltd

JH Clark & Son & Johns Funeral Service

Gichard & Co.

Ronald Hull Jnr Ltd

Lloyd Clough & Sons Ltd

Degussa Fine Organics

KP Nuts

Leger Holidays

E Pawson & Son Ltd

Rotherham College of Arts & Technology

E Russum & Sons Ltd

Rudston Preparatory School

A Ryall & Son (Contractors) Limited

Special Alloys (Northern) Ltd

First published in Great Britain by True North Books Limited
England HX3 6AE
01422 344344

ISBN 1 903204 77 1

Text, design and origination by True North Books Limited
Printed and bound by The Amadeus Press Limited

MEMORIES OF
ROTHERHAM

Contents

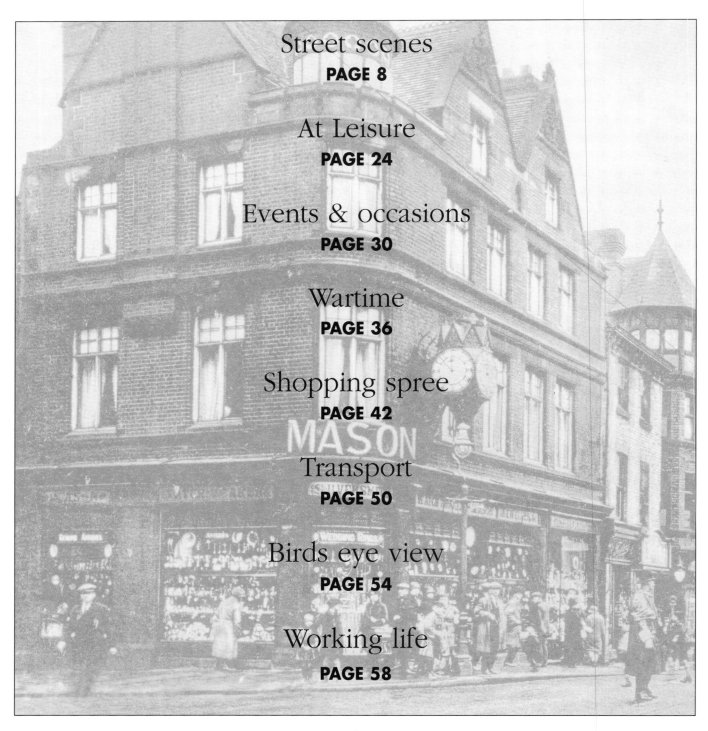

Introduction

Welcome to 'Memories of Rotherham'. You are about to embark upon a magical, mystery tour of nostalgia as we return to the golden days of the middle years of the last century. To enjoy the adventure, all that is needed is a love and a feel for the times of our youth or the days when grandpa was a lad. How those days are referred to depends upon the relative age of the reader, but a common denominator for all of us is an interest in the period that helped mould the face of modern society. This book is not meant to be a definitive history of our town, but a comfortable stroll through the days when cars of any shade, as long as it was black, bowled happily along the far reaching thoroughfare of Effingham Street. We are returning to a time when trolleybuses swung into College Street and dad bought his razor blades at Davy's chemist's on Bridgegate. Mum got her material from Joseph Peck's drapery on Corporation Street and ran up dresses for the girls on her treadle operated Singer sewing machine in the front room. In one single year we experienced three kings on the British throne and, just over half a century ago, watched the coronation of the Queen on flickering black and white television sets. There was the anguish, pain and deprivation of the second world war and its austere aftermath as not everything from that era was a bed of roses. But, we enjoyed the boom of the late 1950s and the fun of the swinging 60s.

It is to those moments in time that the following pages are dedicated. There are stunning photographs to enjoy, each captioned with thoughtful, pithy and even controversial descriptions. Buildings that we had forgotten are brought back to life, along with businesses and places of entertainment that flourished back then. It is possible that the images and comments might settle a few arguments, or they may well provoke some more. Not to worry, for the aim of 'Memories of Rotherham' is that the reader can have his imagination stimulated and his recollections stripped of their cobwebs. Whether the book is to be dipped into or read at a single sitting does not matter, but it is one that will be picked up time and time again. Older generations can reminisce while

younger ones gain a feel of what life was like in their parents' and grandparents' formative years.

Once into the main body of the text and pictures we will be able to trace the pattern of development that helped shape modern Rotherham. However, as this is a turning back of time only as far into the last century as when the Charleston was the dance craze of the day, it is important to consider briefly how our town had reached the point at which the flappers were enjoying themselves. In common with so much of our nation's recorded history, we have the Romans to thank for chronicling reliable information. They came to this area in about 54 AD and, as part of the strategy of subduing local recalcitrant tribes, built a temple and fort close to the River Don. It is from this settlement that the district of Templeborough owes its name. The suffix 'burh' is a Saxon word for a fortified place and the development of the word into 'burgh' or 'borough' is easy to follow. After the Romans left for the sunnier climes of their homeland, the Saxons reigned supreme. After many centuries without a major test of their dominance, their grip on the local administrative controls was fiercely tested by a force of Norsemen, supported by Celtic allies, at the bloody Battle of Brunanburh in 937 AD. Emerging victorious from the carnage at this site between the Don and Rother rivers, the Saxons held sway over much of England until the Norman conquest of 1066. An early mention of our town as Rodreham, the 'homestead on the Rother', can be found in the Domesday Book of 1086.

Rotherham developed slowly as a small market town through the Middle Ages. It was touched by the 17th century English Civil War when it became a Parliamentarian stronghold and boys from the Grammar School fought nobly but unsuccessfully in trying to defend the town bridge against the king's forces. However, it was the founding of Walker's ironworks in the middle of the 18th century and the transformation created by the industrial revolution that altered the life of Rotherham for evermore. In 1801 there were just over 6,000 inhabitants, but the 19th century saw it become part of a continuous industrial belt extending along the Don valley from Sheffield to Mexborough. By the end of the century there were over 54,000 people who called Rotherham home. Employment centred upon the major industries of iron and steel and mining, but also included distilling,

chemicals and glass making. The town was granted borough status in 1902 and now boasts a population across its metropolitan area in excess of 250,000.

The 20th century began as the grand old queen who had reigned for over six decades prepared to breathe her last. As the Victorian era drew to a close, Britain entered a more modern phase of technological development that dramatically altered our environment and the very essence of the way in which we lived. We had already experienced gaslight, but now there would be the wonder of electricity to illuminate homes and power public transport. The first motor cars appeared and man took to the air in powered flight. Radio gave us mass entertainment and information, and cameras recorded everything for posterity. Having painted the background it is now time to apply the finishing brushstrokes with the scenes depicted in 'Memories of Rotherham'. Now there is an opportunity to return to a time when we put silver joeys inside Christmas puddings and sucked on Spangles and gobstoppers. Sing along to Dickie Valentine's 'Finger of suspicion' on that scratchy 78 or chuckle at the exploits of Laurel and Hardy in the 'Film Fun' comic. Put gravy browning on your legs because nylon stockings are not available and tune in to Henry Hall's orchestra on radio's Light Programme. Perm your hair with a Toni or wear it held back by an Alice band. Reach for a Craven A cigarette, 'for your throat's sake' as the adverts told us, and stand up as the headmaster enters the classroom. It is time to turn to the next page and begin a voyage into nostalgia aboard your very own Tardis, whisked off to a time when dad tipped up his pay packet for mum to put into jars labelled 'rent', 'housekeeping', 'milkman', 'insurance' and 'coal'. Let us now go back to an era when people walked on grass rather than smoked it and when offering a seat on a bus to a pretty girl did not get the response, 'What are you after, then?' Return to the days when apples were bought by the pound from a greengrocer and not by the kilo in a supermarket tray encased in polythene. Fifty years or so ago we walked half a mile to school, not a kilometre in a four-by-four driven by a mother who gives birth to a baby and immediately searches for a child minder. Head for that first page of nostalgia and, as waitresses annoyingly say today, 'Enjoy'.

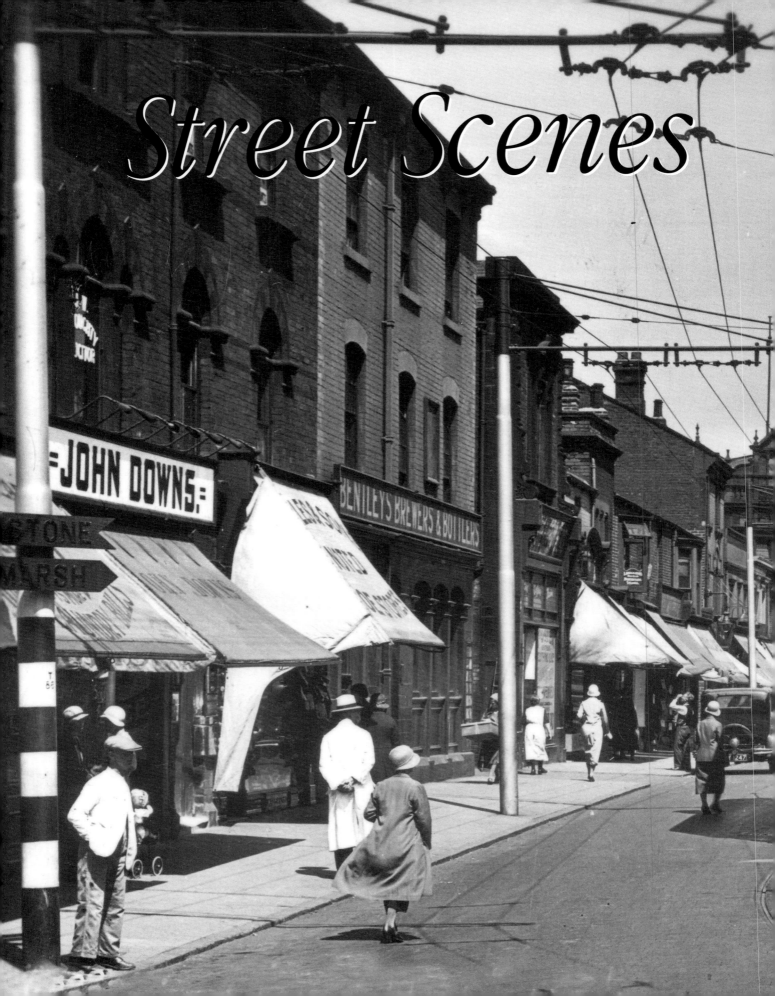

Street Scenes

In the early 1930s the motor car was not the problem that it has become in more recent times. They were the privilege of the middle classes, except when being used by Chicago gangsters standing on the running boards doing battle with Eliot Ness's 'Untouchables'. Looking north along Effingham Street, the women were almost uniformly dressed. Just about every one of them had an identical tight fitting, brimmed hat that shaded the eyes and hid most of the forehead. Men of the era were different. Their headgear tended to reflect social class. Flat caps were for the workers, whereas those with a few shillings in their pockets favoured natty homburgs. Of course, bank managers and the true middle classes went in for bowler hats, but Rotherham did not have too many of that breed. The slimline tram on the left takes the eye, just as much as the curvaceous woman on the pavement in front of it. This was one belonging to Sheffield's fleet. Built by English Electric at Preston, it was one of 11 single ended cars designed by Tom Sykes. They had a driver's cab just at the front, with a rear entrance and stairway, rather than the more usual double ended driving arrangement. This almost unique arrangement worked as the termini at the ends of the route were looped. Even so, when finishing a shift this tram had to be backed along Effingham Street to Rawmarsh Road where the old tram sheds were located.

On Wellgate, long before men went to town
dressed in chinos, jeans or slacks and their
women sported tracksuits, crop tops or T-shirts,
there was something of a uniformity and
formality about the clothing that was worn. In the 1930s
you expected to see a man dressed in a suit, because casual

wear was not a part of his wardrobe. There were working
clothes and those for going out in. An office worker
probably had two suits, one for work and one for best. A
manual worker had his overalls or boiler suit, but mirrored
the white collar employee in having a suit for special
occasions. To be seen out and about on the streets of

Rotherham in anything other than a jacket and trousers was not the done thing. Even the lowest of the low appreciated that. A hat, or flat cap for the workers, was essential. Similarly, women would not dare to go out without their headgear, because only common folk went about bareheaded. The more well-to do-ladies also made sure that they wore gloves, whatever the temperature. Even if you were hard up, at least you could make the effort to look presentable and decent. Quite how those ladies would have viewed today's brigade who display lumps of metal in their belly buttons and garish tattoos on their bodies is anyone's guess.

Above: Russum's brushmakers moved to Tenter Street in 1981, but traded from premises on the left of Bridgegate in the 1930s, as we look towards the parish church and the recently created All Saints Square. This street had been considerably narrower until rewidening in the 1920s took place as most of the buildings on the left hand side were demolished and rebuilt further back. This doubled Bridgegate's width. Today, the east or right hand side of the street provides access to the Cascades, where there was once a narrow entry into New Zealand Yard. Remodelling of this side of Bridgegate in the 1970s removed much of its former 18th century character. Today, there is only one remaining building on the whole street that can claim to be over 200 years old. That is at No 31, next door to where Russum's traded, and is currently a bargain store. At the time of this photograph, it was a furniture shop belonging to James and William Hastings. In the distance, the trolleybus waiting at the Mexborough and Conisbrough stand in the square, ready to turn down into Bridgegate, was one of the Rotherham group of 1929 Guys that worked jointly with the Mexborough and Swinton Traction Company after the scrapping of the trams.

Below: Taken in the 1930s, this view along Effingham Street has changed little in the intervening years. Behind the camera it is a different story as the photographer was positioned with his back to where Boot's now stands, on the fringe of the remodelled shopping area and road system that includes the inner bypass that is Centenary Way. Many of the shops seen here on the left were comparatively recent. They had replaced much earlier properties to bring a more impressive look to this part of town. A branch of Woolworth's opened on this stretch. The company, founded by the American Frank Winfield Woolworth (1852-1919), was part of the changing face of 20th century shopping. The original five and ten cent store came across the Atlantic to Britain in 1909, opening its first branch in Liverpool. Within 25 years most major towns had a 'Woolies' as a fixture. They also seemed to be staffed by young women who were cheerful, but relatively gormless. 'How much is it, love?' they asked, when they should have known the price of the goods they sold. But that was part of the fun and the folklore of the store. The trolleybus at the top of the picture was turning out of College Street on its way to Maltby. This 1931 Ransome was heading towards the Falstaff Inn on the right, near where the trams had their terminus. This hotel, dating from 1869, closed in 1993 and became a branch of Bradford and Bingley.

Bridgegate, as seen from an elevated vantage point in the churchyard, is just as busy a place today as it was over half a century ago. The mock Tudor building on the right is one of the buildings that appeared in the development of the late 1920s. CW Waddington, a tailor and shirtmaker, traded from here until recent years. The entrance yard to the

Red Lion is to its right. This hotel, bearing one of Britain's most popular pub names and the badge of John of Gaunt (1340-99), Duke of Lancaster and son of Edward III, formerly fronted directly onto Bridgegate. Blyth Model Dairies once traded from this block of shops at 43 Bridgegate. It supplied fresh eggs daily that were guaranteed to be graded, tested and clean, straight

from the farm, or so it promised. That was in the days before little lions were stamped or Edwina Currie frightened the nation with her salmonella scare. Other prominent traders here included James and William Hastings, dealers in soft furnishings, furniture and even radiograms, baby carriages and painting and decorating items. This was a well-mixed variety of goods, to say the least. E Russum and Sons, brushmakers, had the premises next to Hastings' outlet. The double decker bus, en route to Chapeltown, stood outside Joseph Peck's. This building is now home to the fast food establishment that is part of the McDonald chain. The Gas Showrooms, in the distance on Frederick Street, are now an entrance area for the bus station.

Above: The 1920s were supposed to be an era of rebuilding after the horrors of the Great War. They turned out to be something rather different. Although some redevelopment took place, that decade is best remembered for depression, strikes and the stock market crash. The scene was often one of people standing around with nothing to do, a little like some of those depicted in this photograph of Bridgegate from the late 20s. Seen from the junction with Chantry Bridge and Frederick Street, the photographer stood with his back to Rotherham Bridge and its almost unique Chapel on the Bridge, one of only three such places of worship in England. Part of the right hand side of Bridgegate had been redeveloped and those further up on the left, in front of All Saints' Church, would soon go to create All Saints Square. On the near corner, George Thompson and Sons traded as outfitters, across from the County Borough. This hostelry, in its original form, opened as the Restaurant Inn in 1859. One of its owners included Lydia Law, the founder of Rotherham Girls' School, a somewhat disparate mixture of interests. Perhaps she promoted crème de menthe as much as la crème de la crème of Miss Jean Brodie! The construction of Corporation Street just before the first world war led to the rebuilding of the inn and it was reopened as the County Borough in honour of Rotherham's status when it was elevated on 1 October 1902. Sharp-eyed readers might be able to make out Davy's chemists and Russum's famous hanging brush sign on the left.

Top right: Almost completely unrecognisable today, this was Effingham Square, looking down Effingham Street and away from the town centre towards Grafton Bridge. The group of men looking towards the camera in this photograph from the early 1930s might have enjoyed a tipple in the Grey Horse Inn, on the left by Drummond Street. It had originally been known as the Merry Heart, opening as such in 1862. It finally closed its doors almost exactly a century later on 25 February 1962. Behind the men, Albert Handley's shop dealt in linoleum, a cheap and hardwearing floor covering that was used in most homes as carpeting was far too expensive. Anyone with a Wilton made sure that it was reserved for the front room. Perhaps the people featured near the clock were waiting for a bus to Silverwood colliery, as this was the terminus for that service. Popularly known as the 'Four clocks', the Hastings Clock stood here for over 50 years. It was gifted to the town by businessman James Hastings and unveiled on 20 June 1912 to commemorate the coronation of George V a year earlier. The clock was dismantled in 1961 when the square was redeveloped, but was replaced next to the Civic Building, close to its original position, in 1969.

Far right: This sweep of road takes us along College Street and into Effingham Street and All Saints Square, as they looked in the early 1930s. On the left was the drapery store belonging to Joseph Smith and Sons. This part of town was well blessed with drapers and outfitters. On the same block as Smith's, Frederick Gilling and William Cottam had shops conducting similar business. Melia's was sandwiched between Smith's and Gilling's. This shop was a grocer's, styling itself as a provisions dealer. Across

the road were the two growing giants that could soon be found in every town centre up and down the land. Interestingly, at the time they were described as 'bazaars' in official trade directories. This word had been apt when referring to Woolworth's and Marks and Spencer's in their earlier days, but they had both moved on from their humble origins. Frank Woolworth founded his first store in America in 1879 and the company came to Rotherham in the late 1920s. Marks and Spencer moved into the former Grapes Inn building in 1932. Michael Marks had run penny bazaars in Leeds, but branched out into a more distinguished field after joining forces with Thomas Spencer in 1894 in the market hall in Wigan.

Below: During the 1930s there was an awful lot of standing around to be done, as instanced by some of the men in this view along the length of Bridgegate from Frederick Street and Corporation Street to the parish church. There was employment in the coalfields and the iron and steel industry, but not for everyone. The depression of the late 1920s and early 1930s hit hard for the ordinary man in the street. Those actually in work found that they had periods on short time, their pay packets were slimmer and the hours grew longer. For those without employment, it was a grim time. Families and friends helped out where they could, but it was the dickens of a job trying to make ends meet. The rent man was dodged, the kids were on bread and jam and loan sharks made a killing. In 1931 the Labour Government introduced cuts in unemployment benefit and raised taxes as Britain's gold reserves dwindled. Crime figures, especially for larceny, rose as people sought foul means as well as fair to put food on the table. There were riots in our cities and hunger marchers from Lancashire descended on the capital in late 1932. As we got further into the decade, things improved not a jot. In October 1936 hundreds set off from Jarrow to march on London and petition the government, only to be snubbed by the arrogant prime minister, Stanley Baldwin.

Bottom right: Standing in All Saints' churchyard, the camera was pointed across the square towards John Law and Sons and down Bridgegate, with the access to Upper Millgate to the left. The bus driver and conductor were wearing their regulation red-trimmed khaki warehouse coats and company caps as they waited for the appropriate moment to set off on their next journey. In the meantime, they commented on the current affairs that affected them in c1930. They were happy to be in work, as so many of their friends and family were on the dole. This state of affairs was not what had been promised a dozen years earlier. At the end of World War I the government promised that it would make the nation a place fit for heroes to live in. As so many sacrifices had been made in the cockpit of Europe it was only right that Britain should honour its citizens with a better standard of living. Yet, this pair discussing the state of the nation must have wondered if Prime Minister Lloyd George had really known how empty his words were. Even after the Great War finished we were still fighting a civil war with the Irish. Children continued to go hungry and, with riots on the streets, there was strife everywhere. By 1930 there were 2,000,000 out of work: a figure that would continue to rise over the next few years.

Above right: The finger that is the spire of the parish church pointed heavenwards in this delightful early 1930s view of the bus station in All Saints Square. It served as the central terminal until 1971 before moving to its present site off Frederick Street. The bus in the foreground was a 1927 ADC,

belonging to East Midland, and was painted in an attractive chocolate, cream and chrome yellow scheme. Davy's Café, on the left, advertised its 'delicious tea and coffee'. It was very handily placed and did a roaring trade as people rested their limbs after a hard day's shopping or office work as they waited for their bus to come and whisk them off home for their evening meal. Quite often the day started with a cuppa at Arthur Davy and Sons in order to set up the body for the rigours that lay ahead. It was also a good place in which to catch up on the latest gossip. Who knows which husband with the wrong wife might happen to come through the doors? And, what about that chap in the pinstriped suit? Do not tell me that the young woman gazing into his eyes is his niece. You got more than refreshment on a visit to Davy's Café; it was also a window on the world.

Above: Ward's Ales was a champion Sheffield brew on sale at the Old College Inn that dominated the Effingham Street end of All Saints Square in the late 1940s. Men drank from pint glasses and not straight from the bottle with a mobile phone affixed to their ears as seems to be the style of the new millennium. Ladies were content to partake of a port and lemon or sweet sherry rather than quaff pints of lager or brightly coloured alcopops. Although Ward's closed its brewery doors at the turn of the century, there was good news some years later when, in 2004, Cumbria's Jennings' brewery announced that it was relaunching the famous name. We can all say 'Cheers!' to that news. Until Ward's rebuilt the pub in 1930, it was known just as the College Inn since it opened its doors at 23 College Street in 1822. It finally closed on 2 December 1970. It was not only drinkers who enjoyed entering the premises. The second floor was a billiard hall and many a cannon or an in-off was played on its tables over the years. As snooker displaced billiards in popularity, many was the waistcoated young man with visions of emulating John Pullman or Fred Davis as he practised the arts of stun, screw and side. The buses by the stand provide a touch of amusement. The trolley on the left has tapering letters for its destination of Thrybergh Park Lane so that they can fit into the small aperture. The bus was not going to be damaged by being allowed to run away. A scotch or wedge of wood, attached to a chain, was positioned by the front offside wheel.

Below: In 1949 we used public transport to get around. Private motoring was expensive and the austere postwar years meant that we had to tighten our belts as certain goods were still rationed and the country had a huge war debt to pay off. No wonder that the man in the street grumbled about who had really won the war. Peacetime was anything but cosy, but at least he did not have to suffer the daily risk to life and limb that lasted for six long, terrifying years. College Street was subject to much redevelopment in the interwar years. Stores that were to become household names submitted plans to develop sites in the area. In 1927 Burton's, the 'tailor of taste', arrived, to be followed by Woolworth's the following year. In 1932, Marks and Spencer opened its doors. This street, once Brookgate, was named after the College of Jesus, built by Thomas Rotherham, a former Lord Chancellor and Archbishop of York in the 15th century. The tram in the picture had seen better days. Built in the mid 1930s, it was on its way up towards High Street and out to Templeborough. The driver standing at the controls would not be required to make many more journeys as this form of transport ceased to run on this route after 11 November 1949. This was an apt date for its demise as it coincided with the day dedicated to the memory of those whose lives ended in two world wars.

Below: On Henry Street in 1960 the Hippodrome was in the process of being demolished, having closed the previous year. The last double bill, shown on 19 December 1959, was a forgettable coupling of 'When the devil drives', starring Francoise Arnoul, and 'Runaway daughters', both 'X' certificate movies. This grubby pairing was a poor reflection on a grand building with a fine reputation in Rotherham entertainment. It opened on 3 August 1908 as a theatre presenting variety turns. Designed by the Leeds architects Chadwick and Watson, it had a 2,500 capacity and within its Italian renaissance façade there twinkled 1,400 electric lights. A private box would set you back half a guinea, but a humble seat in the gods cost just thruppence. The Hippodrome was not the town's first theatre. That honour belonged to the Alexandra Music Hall and Theatre of Varieties on Howard Street that opened on 7 November 1870 with such delightfully described acts as duettists and dialogue artistes, an Ethiopian delineator, step dancers, an electric acrobat and a dancing comic. The mind boggles! The Hippodrome continued the practice of bringing top names to Rotherham, with the likes of Gracie Fields and George Formby appearing on stage. It converted to a cinema in 1932 and on 17 October showed its first film, 'No limit', starring the debonair French musical comedy star, Maurice Chevalier, and Clara Bow, the 'It girl' who never was 'it' in talkies because of her pronounced Brooklyn accent.

Above: Hardly a square inch of pavement can be seen on Frederick Street. Stretching down towards Chapel Bridge, a vast sea of humanity queues to wait for a series of trolley-buses and trams making their way along the road to carry the multitude to its destination. Probably dating from the late 1940s, there is no record of the destination of these people. It is, perhaps, not too fanciful to suggest that some sporting attraction was the object of their patience, waiting as they were in such numbers for the next vehicle to arrive. Deprived of a diet of professional sport during the war, the first few years of peacetime saw a surge in attendances at various venues. Soccer grounds were full to overflowing and cricket lovers waited for hours before seeing a ball being bowled, so anxious were they to get through the turnstiles in good time. Speedway flourished and rugby was played in front of full houses. Perhaps Doncaster Racecourse was a more likely destination, as the No 77 bus went this way. The Mexborough and Swinton trolleybus approaching Chapel Bridge sported its distinctive two tone livery. This company was known to locals as the 'M & S' and is the only business to have ever rivalled the town centre chain store for such familiarity. The shed like building in the distance belonged to the Rotherham Forge and Rolling Mills.

Above: The town library is now housed with the Arts Centre, close to the Civic Offices at Walker Place. The somewhat foreboding architecture of the present structure, typical of late 60s and early 70s utilitarian design, belies a more attractive interior staffed by librarians who are keen to please and happy to share their knowledge with the general public. What a refreshing change that is from the harridans in reference libraries and archives elsewhere who regard all the books as their own and only allow access to them one at a time after the reader has undergone a security check worthy of an American airport. Rotherham's first public library was based in an imposing building situated on the corner of Market Street and Main Street that shared its facilities with the municipal baths. It opened on 20 June 1887, even though work on it was not fully completed until January 1888. The senior librarian insisted that the price of each book was written inside so that borrowers could appreciate the full value of the words they were reading! The library was badly damaged in a fire in 1925 and it was not until 1931 that this new one on Howard Street, pictured after a scaffolding collapse on 23 May 1962, was opened to the public. It is typical of our fascination with accidents and disasters that a crowd soon appeared to view what was just a pile of twisted steel rods and a couple of dented vehicles.

Below: In 1963 there were three main categories of films, as determined by the board of film censors. 'X' was reserved for movies deemed to be too scary or steamy for the under 16s, but 'U' stood for 'universal' and there were no restrictions on audiences for showing such as 'Samson and the 7 miracles', featuring Gordon Scott and Yoko Tani. However, it was screened in a pairing with 'Reptilicus', starring Carl Ottosen and Ann Smyrner, that attracted an 'A' certificate that meant children had to be accompanied by an adult to gain admission. You would have to be the keenest of movie buffs or be related to Barry Norman to recall these movies or their stars. Future attractions of 'Tyrant of Syracuse' and 'Drums of Africa' sounded similarly unappealing offerings by the Cinema House, Doncaster Gate. When it opened on 9 March 1914, a ladies' orchestra, led by Mrs Victor Haydn, entertained customers. How typical of the time that she had to use her husband's Christian name. The cinema's Moorish façade was topped by four domes and was designed by WG Beck of Sheffield. How elegant it was to take tea in the grand café. The first film shown sounded like a real thriller as it was called 'Tower of Terror'. The Cinema House was remodelled several times in the 1930s and early 1950s before running its last reel in 1964. It became a bingo hall, as did so many during that decade.

At Leisure

Simple pleasures can keep children engrossed for hours, whatever the era. They are also especially happy when there is anything messy or an element of risk can be introduced. Here they had the best of both worlds. Paddling through the mud and water, the pair on the swingboat had a whale of a time pretending to be captains of a ship as they swayed precariously above the gentle waters lapping beneath their feet. Elsewhere, people were not so joyous as the floods of 1931 caused some damage to homes and property. Poor families could ill afford to see their possessions ruined because many of them were without insurance as the premiums were too much for their meagre resources. This was beyond the understanding of the youngsters in the Rotherham Road recreation ground, Parkgate. They just wanted to have some fun and get their knees dirty. Playing on the 'rec' was part of growing up, along with climbing trees, playing rally-o in the street, having conker battles and swinging on a rope above the river. Girls played jacks and two ball, while lads mooched about collecting tadpoles or annoying neighbours by knocking on doors and running away. It would be good to see some of our young ones today learning about a top and whip, hopscotch or the simple pleasures of blow football.

It takes little effort to get from the town centre to Clifton Park. Just a stroll down Doncaster Gate and onto Doncaster Road and you are there. Even though it is so near to the hustle and bustle of the retail world, you would think that you had travelled to a different planet, full of verdant lawns, shady trees and flowers in full bloom. In the foreground two lovely little tots pluck at the daisies and soon will be asking for help in forming them into chains to garland their necks. They will tickle each other's chins with buttercups while their mums enjoy a chinwag in the shadow of the bandstand. Memories of colliery bands and the Salvation Army blowing fit to burst come flooding back. Old Sousa marches and songs from the shows can be imagined drifting across the park and Rossini's 'William Tell' could be trumpeted without anyone thinking of the Lone Ranger. This bandstand was erected in 1928, replacing a cast iron one that had lasted until 1919. After World War II, bands played dance music on Sunday nights and older female readers may well recall the lads who trod on their toes attempting a spin turn in the waltz. A new bandstand was opened in 1991 by Queen Elizabeth II to mark Clifton Park's centenary.

Below: Before the second world war we had got used to taking our holidays by the sea. Scarborough, Bridlington, Cleethorpes, Skegness, Cromer and Mablethorpe all had their fans and it was a welcome break from working down the mines or in the iron and steel works if you could get a week or two in a guest house, even if the landlady was rather formidable. Some families were so taken with a particular resort that, as they left at the end of their holiday, they rebooked for the following year with the same proprietor. A lot of that changed in the early 1940s. With the war dominating everything, precious fuel had to be conserved for essential transport. Every trip to the coast meant less fuel for the armoured cars and trains that were steaming along pulling carriages full of troops or wagons laden with ordnance. Rationing of fuel and food made things doubly difficult, but the government recognised the need to keep the nation's morale at a high level. Consequently, local councils were encouraged to organise activities under a 'holidays at home' scheme. Families came into Clifton Park and got all the fun of the fair, plus Punch and Judy men and beauty contests to help them forget their worries for a while. It was not quite as good as strolling along the prom, but at least it was something.

Above: In the 1950s Jane Morgan sang about 'The day that the rains came down'. They certainly did on Sheffield Road. Front gardens were flooded and, unfortunately, so were parlours and hallways. Families did their best to move furniture upstairs, but damage to lino and carpets was difficult to avoid. Then there was the smell that seemed to linger for weeks and turned even the strongest of stomachs. The children made the best of the situation. Out came the wellies and off the kiddies went for a good old splash and paddle. Naughty boys stamped hard and made their sisters squeal out loudly, 'Tell him, mum!' That, of course, only hardened their brothers' resolve. Middle-aged readers might recognise themselves or their look-alikes in this photograph. This was a period when children had knees. Boys wore short trousers and girls had skirts or dresses. Short sleeved jumpers, lovingly knitted by mum or gran, invariably had hooped or striped patterns. Shirts were grey or cream. We often wore short ankle socks, but made a concession made to the winter months by donning ones that reached just below knees that were permanently scabbed from playground tumbles. When it got really cold we had to wear balaclavas to keep our ears and head warm and protect our chapped faces from the chilly wind.

Above: He was born South Carolina in 1941 and christened Ernest Evans. As a teenager he was a fan of rock and roll's Fats Domino and, on becoming a singer, adapted that name to Chubby Checker. When he recorded 'The twist' in 1960 and followed it with 'Let's twist again' in 1961, he inspired a dance craze that swept across the ballroom floors on either side of the Atlantic. For the first time ever, couples danced without touching one another. It was even possible to dance alone and gyrating bodies bobbing up and down became a common sight in every dancehall. Other singers cashed in on the craze and even such more middle-of-the-road stalwarts as Petula Clark and Frankie Vaughan had hits with 'Ya ya twist' and 'Don't stop, twist', respectively. Fairgrounds saw a chance to freshen up their image, as instanced by the slogan above the waltzers on Main Street on 28 April 1962 during the Spring Fair. The cars hurtled from side to side, with squealing girls clutching the safety bars, as swarthy youths that mum had warned us about gave a little extra push to heighten the fear factor. 'Do you remember when things were really humming?' as Chubby asked. Well, we certainly did as we staggered off the ride dizzy, but elated by the experience.

Below: It was hardly the same as the sands at Sutton on sea, but during the second world war we often had to make do with holidays at home. Clifton Park provided as many attractions as it possibly could to help us imagine that we really were 'on our hols'. There were roundabouts and sideshows, plus that speciality of the British beach - the donkey ride. Children tried to imagine that they were Gordon Richards or Harry Wragg as the told their mounts to 'Gee up'. But, the donkeys had heard it all before. They sauntered along at their own sedate rate, led by their owner who had taken thousands of pennies in his time from parents who were just happy to see their young ones having fun. In this wartime photo, the man in charge of donkey rides seems to be having words with the lad whose socks are at half mast. He would not have been adverse to giving the boy a bit more than a flea in his ear by the look of his body language. Still, he had the best answer to any lip he was being given. There would be no ride for this young scamp until he learned some manners. In the 1940s children did as they were told and were not expected to talk back to their elders.

Events & occasions

Never mind health and safety with its restrictions on how we now conduct our lives, there was something more important at stake in 1945. At last we could be carefree. Following devastating atomic bomb attacks on Nagasaki and Hiroshima earlier in the month, on 14 August Japan unconditionally surrendered to bring to an end to the second world war. People literally pushed the boat out in celebration. The high jinks did not quite match the joy of VE Day in May, but there were still plenty of parties and celebrations held. At Aldwarke on 22 August workers from the colliery and steel works took their families on a trip down the Sheffield and South

Yorkshire Navigation. The 'Rowland', a barge built for canal carriers Waddington and Sons of Swinton, was pressed into service as a pleasure craft. Gay bunting and Union flags fluttered in the breeze as passengers enjoyed the moment. The 'Rowland' usually carried glassworks, but it had a more precious cargo on this occasion that included the children who would be our hope for the future. This barge was the first petrol powered craft of its type on the canal having been fitted with an engine taken from a Buick motor car. In medieval times Aldwarke was an estate associated with the Clarell, Fitzwilliam and Fojambe families, but in 1945 it was at the heart of the town's heavy industry.

Below: The very last pit pony to see work in the Rotherham area led a parade down High Street, Rawmarsh in c1958. Hopefully, it was off to have a long and well deserved retirement by being put out to grass. This hardy beast toiled in the mines pulling heavy coal tubs along the rails in what must have been a tough life. Many of those used in mining were bred from Welsh ponies, a breed originating in the mountains and specially developed to work in this industry. Not all ponies conformed to the cartoonist Thelwell's idealism of chubby steeds with girlie riders performing at a gymkhana. Coal mining was one of our most important industries during the 19th and most of the 20th century. Locally, the first workings were on outcrops on the hillside. Mine shafts were sunk in the 18th century and the coming of the canal system meant that the fuel could be moved considerable distances. However, the coming of the railway provided a greater impetus because it enabled goods to be moved more quickly and in greater volume. As demand grew, deeper shafts were sunk and mines expanded. Industry in neighbouring towns and cities, notably Sheffield steel, depended upon Rotherham coal. Earl Fitzwilliam improved the transport connections between his Rawmarsh collieries and Sheffield by promoting the Sheffield and Rotherham Railway.

Right: Despite the message on the decorated trolleybus in All Saints Square, it was the coronation of the king that we celebrated on 12 May 1937. However, his wife, the former Elizabeth Bowes-Lyon (1900-2002), was already a popular figure with the general public. She was the first consort for centuries to hail from a British family, following a string of German and Danish princes and princesses who had married into our royal families. The celebrations for George VI's enthronement contained an element of relief mixed in with the gaiety. The previous year had given us three kings who included the controversial Edward VIII. Thanks to his notorious affair with the twice-divorced American socialite, Wallis Simpson, the establishment was thrown into crisis when he announced his intention to make her his wife. The general public at home knew little of the long-running saga, though continental and American newspapers had been full of gossip for several years. Matters came to a head in late 1936 and resulted in the king's abdication. Debate about the rights and wrongs of his relationship continued for a while, but soon the country rallied behind the new monarch, a nervous and hesitant man thrown into a spotlight he did not relish. His coronation took place on the date originally earmarked for his brother's official enthronement.

Above right: In 1908 the first shaft was sunk at Maltby Main Colliery, situated on the Tickhill Road to the east of the township. It was one of several mines to open in South Yorkshire either side of World War I. This colliery benefited from rich seams of coal deposits and had a good production record. The pit company commissioned the building of Maltby Model Village from c1910 onwards to attract and house the workforce. About 1,000 houses were built, radiating out along two concentric circles of roads. This

approach to house building avoided the creation of high density terraces prevalent in other mining communities. In the census of 1891 Maltby's population numbered just 709, but by 1921 it had risen to 7,500 and stood at over 10,000 a decade later. But mining is a dangerous job. On 28 July 1923 an explosion killed 27 men at Maltby Main. In this scene from 1947, the year that the National Coal Board was formed, we had one of the toughest winters on record with freezing temperatures at the same time as widespread power cuts. It was also time to record another accident at the mine. The funeral procession for one more underground victim wound its way slowly to the cemetery. Fellow workers showed their solidarity and turned out in their hundreds, but it would not be the last mining fatality Britain would experience in 1947. In mid August 104 perished at the William Pit in Whitehaven.

Below: Although the photograph is undated it would not have taken Sexton Blake or Paul Temple more than a moment to determine that this jolly group of children must have posed for the camera in June 1953. The bunting above their heads and the picture of a young Queen Elizabeth II strongly suggest that these were part of the coronation celebrations taking place all over Britain at that time. The school maypole dancers were from Aston Fence, on the Sheffield Road. They had been rehearsing for weeks and performed a traditional folk dance, moving in and out as they wove ribbons up and down the pole, cavorting in front of an enchanted set of parents and school chums. Their teacher watched anxiously in case one of the less well co-ordinated, usually a boy, managed to throttle himself as he went under instead of over. Such dances are survivals of ancient ones around a living tree as part of spring rites to ensure fertility, but Miss did not use such basic words to describe the activity or too many awkward questions might have been asked. The youngsters each received a commemorative five shilling crowns, set in a plastic case, and the coronation mug they also received would have pride of place on the mantelpiece for years to come.

Right: How proudly the parents were of their children parading along the street at Kilnhurst, just southeast of Swinton. There was a mixture of best clothes, fancy dress and Brownie uniforms in this section of the procession. Gap-toothed youngsters grinned at the camera as their mums and dads puffed out their chests with pride. Streamers and flags were everywhere, looking very jolly on this special day in 1935. It was the first national celebration since the end of the first world war, over 16 years earlier. King George V acceded to the throne in 1910 and on 6 May the country acknowledged his silver jubilee with parades, parties and firework displays. It must have a poignant moment for our monarch because the festivities surrounding his 25th anniversary also marked the day upon which his father, Edward VII, had died from pneumonia. It is interesting to note that our own Queen Elizabeth II celebrated her silver and golden jubilees in the summertime and not in February, the true anniversary of her father's demise. The crowds that turned out in 1977 and 2002 showed how popular she is and the same was true for her grandfather. He was well-loved by his subjects who appreciated his blunt and direct manner. They also remembered that he had jettisoned the Germanic Saxe-Coburg-Gotha family name in 1917, replacing it with Windsor, and applauded him for doing so.

Wartime

Below: The steelworks at Templeborough was a prime target for enemy bombers, but anything else in the vicinity was fair game as far as they were concerned. Rotherham experienced attack from the skies during the first world war when Zeppelins flew overhead, but the damage they caused was little in comparison to what was unleashed nearly a quarter of a century later. The first major blast in this area occurred on the night of 28/29 August 1940. The town centre and surrounding properties were damaged as the hail of death rained down seemingly unabated. Residents took to the Anderson shelters and shivered in fear, wincing with each explosion, until the all-clear was sounded. Those living on Josephine Road, Masbrough returned to find a scene of destruction and devastation that haunted them for the rest of their lives. It was not just bricks and mortar that were lost, these were people's homes that were full of personal possessions and fond memories. They wept more over the loss of a grandmother's photograph or baby's first teddy than for any armchair, table or bed that had been blown to smithereens. The offices and stables at Midland Iron Works were also badly affected. In total, Rotherham and district experienced 142 air raids during the war, most of them as a result of secondary action when Sheffield was the main focus. On 12 December 1940 there was an alert that lasted for over nine hours and in 1942 an attack was made on Clifton Park when the Luftwaffe presumably mistook the Holidays at Home tents for an army encampment.

Below: Party hats were made from any scraps of paper that had not been handed in during the salvage drives of World War II. Flags and bunting left over from the 1937 coronation were pressed into service and flown across York Road and every similar street in the country when news filtered through on 8 May 1945 that the enemy had laid down its arms and the war in Europe was over. Victory in Europe Day, or VE Day as it soon became known, became part of British folklore as the occasion when the nation went wild with joy. Impromptu congas and hokey-cokeys were danced In All Saints Square, bobbies' helmets were stuck on top of lampposts, the royal family was cheered by thousands outside Buckingham Palace and cries of 'Good old Winnie' greeted the prime minister wherever he went as he raise his familiar two fingered victory salute. Trestle tables, commandeered from church and school halls, were dragged out into the street. Mums donned their pinnies and used up a week's worth of valuable ration coupons in staging the best party the children had ever experienced. There were smiles back upon everyone's faces for the first time in six years, though when the festivities came to an end there were some who went back inside and shed a quiet tear for a husband or lover who would never experience the happiness that his ultimate sacrifice had made possible.

Below: Protective clothing and tools of the trade were limited to a tin hat each, a hand pump and hose and a couple of gardening implements. With such equipment this family was all set to go on its fire watching duties.

Pictured outside 33 Ramsden Road in 1940, it is easy for a sophisticate from the 21st century to pour scorn on these people and their attempts to contribute to the Air Raid Precautions (ARP) service. What should be

happening is that homage be given to these brave souls who put their own welfare second to the greater good. They knew they had to do their bit for the war effort. Not everyone could don a uniform and march off to fight the foe. Some were needed to keep the wheels of industry turning, while others had to produce the food we needed from our own land as the U-boats blockaded our coastline and prevented convoy ships from getting through. Civil defence presented opportunities for those too old or too young to join up. The Ramsden Road family became part of a group that Churchill was later to refer to as 'the army that Hitler forgot'. Mum, dad and the children were out and about when the bombs were falling and provided invaluable backup to the fire crews tackling the blazes caused when the Luftwaffe's bombers struck.

Top: Boys will be boys and these little monkeys were having great fun pretending to be soldiers, much to the amusement of two artillerymen watching them from the Drill Hall on Fitzwilliam Road. Lads have always loved to play with toy guns and here they had made use of bits of piping and wooden staves in their fantasy of being soldiers at drill. Their older brothers indulged in the real thing, because there was a war on. These boys would still have been too young to join up when the war ended in 1945, but each one of them would be related to or know someone who was in uniform and fighting on some foreign field, manning a battleship's guns or setting off on a bombing raid over Germany. Their lives would be touched with sadness if they saw the postman bringing the telegram that began, 'I regret to inform you ...' because that meant there would be yet one more who was not coming home. Our six make-believe soldiers were good pals. For the men at the front it was in the darkest hours of World War II that many lasting friendships were formed, even if it was hard to be very pally with someone who might not be there the following day.

Right: The corporal of this Home Guard platoon received a small trophy, but we can only guess at whether this was a personal or team award. All we can be sure of is that every single one of these fellows deserved a cup for the effort they put in. Some were of the wrong age to join up, had an infirmity or held reserved occupations, but they were united in their intention to serve their country as best they could, despite being denied call up papers. When it was first decided to form an army, originally called Local Defence Volunteers (LDV) and drawn mainly from the ranks of the over 40s, those who came forward were the objects of some scorn. Poorly equipped, they often had to drill with broomsticks and shovels instead of rifles. Cynics said that they were playing at being soldiers and doubted the value that they would have if ever the enemy invaded. Winston Churchill helped change attitudes. First of all the prime minister renamed the LDV as the Home Guard in the summer of 1941. Idiotic ideas such as launching petrol bombs by catapult or stretching piano wire across a road to decapitate a German motorcyclist were abandoned. Proper weapons and uniforms were issued and training was profes-

sionally conducted. The Home Guard became increasingly effective, watching over key installations, releasing regular units for active duties and demonstrating the true value of local knowledge on manoeuvres.

Bottom left: They look a little weary and were probably taking a rest during a tour of duty that stretched their meagre resources to the limit. Although the equipment may not have been of the highest specification, there was little doubt about their determined resolve to play their part in protecting life and property. Driven by a mixture of fear and fury, they served their country well. This sextet of volunteer firemen gathered around a Coventry Climax trailer pump on the river bank at Ickles. During World War II it was their job to tackle any blazes at the Steel, Peech and Tozer plant. Wearing their protective gear, they were ready to deal with anything that might erupt after Herman Goering's Luftwaffe bombers dropped their incendiaries. Alerts were frequent, especially during 1940-41 when the blitz upon our industry, homes and heritage was at its worst. The steelworks was always likely to be a target for the Heinkels and Junkers that brought their deadly load to the region. Although Rotherham suffered less than many similar towns, it was always on the alert and relied heavily on brave souls, such as those seen here, who were willing to tackle the fires as bombs and masonry continued to fall around their ears. The Templeborough works were important to the war effort as local steel production provided shells, tanks and wheels. The melting shop, the largest of its type in Europe, was nicknamed 'the anvil of South Yorkshire'.

Below: Although this photograph is dated December 1940, this is probably incorrect by 12 months. Princess Louise, Duchess of Argyll died on 3 December 1939 at the age of 91. Her great niece, wearing the black armband, would not have been in mourning a year later. Seen shaking hands with Lady Lawson-Tancred, wife of Sir Thomas the 9th Baronet, Mary, the Princess Royal and great aunt of Anne, the current holder of the title, had arrived at Westgate Station to review the local Auxiliary Territorial Service (ATS) and Women's Voluntary Service (WVS). Princess Mary (1897-1965) was King George V's only daughter and was actually born Victoria Alexandra Alice Mary. During World War I she visited hospitals and welfare organisations, assisting with projects to give comfort to British servicemen and assistance to their families. In 1922 she married Viscount Lascelles, later to be the 6th Earl of Harewood. At the outbreak of World War II the Princess Royal became chief controller and later controller commandant of the ATS, renamed the Women's Royal Army Corp in 1949. In that capacity she travelled Britain visiting its units, as well as wartime canteens and other welfare groups that included the WVS, the civil defence organisation founded in 1938. The WVS was the brainchild of Stella, Lady Reading who had been at the heart of the Personal Service League of the early 30s that helped families adversely affected by the depression years. The WVS gained official royal approval in 1966, becoming the Women's Royal Voluntary Service.

Shopping spree

Until Corporation Street was built in 1913 this top end of High Street was a problematic bottleneck for traffic, even in those far off days. Although the rest of the street below has suffered in recent years and taken on a jaded appearance, Mason's building still stands as testament to the imagination and art of our ancestral architects and builders. Dating from the 1760s, its cupolas, turrets and crafted façade stand out as a lesson to modern town planners. Can you really imagine that anyone a quarter of a millennium hence will admire or want to preserve the concrete, steel and glass rubbish that passes for architecture these days? There is little chance of it surviving, anyway, in this throwaway society in which we live. The clock on Mason's jeweller's had formerly hung outside the Daily Express building in Fleet Street and was moved to adorn the shop just after the first world war. The old clockwork mechanism was sited in the basement, controlling the hands via a complicated series of rods. It was electrified in 1965. John Mason came to Rotherham from Worksop in 1854 and, after holding premises further down High Street, moved into No 36 in 1883. Mason was the town mayor in 1888-89 and his jeweller's has long been a landmark in the town. It was only in the early 21st century that the business changed hands. It is now a shoe shop, run by Christopher Hamby. Coincidentally, there is still a jeweller's in this vicinity as Clive's trades just next door.

Right: All Saints Square was created in 1933 when property between the churchyard and College Street was demolished. The whole square was pedestrianised in 1971 and now acts as an attractive focal point for shoppers catching their breath on the benches close to the little water feature. In May 1965, it was a different story as buses brought families into the town centre, making it a busy thoroughfare for traffic and pedestrians alike. The blue and cream bus stop sign belonged to the Rotherham Corporation company that, by this time, had almost completely replaced its trolleybuses with motorised ones. By October the 'trackless trams' would have disappeared completely. One of the last of their type was approaching the platform on its way to the Pumping Station via Corporation Street. The 22 bus from All Saints Square to Braithwell's Red Lion took just under the half hour to complete its journey at a princely cost of a shilling (5p). The crowds out and about during this month could have given a thought to events happening at Runnymede, close to where the Magna Carta was signed. The Queen dedicated an area of wood and grassland to the memory of John F Kennedy, the American president so cruelly assassinated in late 1963. His beautiful widow, Jacque-line, attended the ceremony and our hearts went out to her as we recalled those poignant and heart moving images of her cradling her dying husband's head in the rear of the presidential limousine on that awful day in Dallas.

Bottom left: Fairs and markets were important in establishing the status of a town. Rotherham's first charter, granted in 1207 during the reign of King John, gave Eustace de Veci the right to hold a two day fair during the feast of St Edmund. This fair became known as the Statutes and was an annual event until 1978. Richard de Waddesly got permission to hold a weekly market thanks to a charter granted exactly a century later. Later, the markets were owned by the Feoffees, a form of governing body that oversaw road construction and the care of the sick and needy, which continued to control them until 1801. In c1950 the town market hall, on the left as we look along Corporation Street, had its origins in the charters that had been granted centuries before. The first hall opened in April 1879, but was badly damaged by fire on 21 January 1888. It was then discovered that only £800 worth of insurance was in force to offset the £6,500 damage! The new market, designed by Archibald Neill of Leeds, opened on 18 December 1889 and functioned until 1971, the site becoming a car park. The National Provincial Bank, now NatWest, can be seen on the corner with Market Street. The white building above belonged to EJ Brown, a long established ironmonger.

Below: It looks to be a lovely summer's day c1950 as we look across All Saints Square towards the Old College Inn. On the right a couple of schoolgirls follow their mother away from the bus stand. Dressed in their light summer frocks, they would have appreciated not having to bother with heavy blazers on a day like this. It is interesting to note that many schools have returned to having a set uniform in recent times. From the start of the 1970s, when comprehensive education became the rage, a certain relaxing of rules came into being. Some thought it only right in the days of flower power and equality, but reactionaries regarded it as the first step on the slippery, downward slope to laissez-faire land. Perhaps the fuddy-duddies were right after all, because many modern parents have decided that uniforms for schoolchildren are a good thing. Do they realise that everyone thought like that once? Also making a comeback is getting youngsters to do some homework, even at an early age. Our featured girls would have been well used to that. They had 'times tables' to learn and spelling lists to grapple with when they got home because there would be a test the following day.

Above: Let us hope that the photographer had permission from the vicar to trample over the remains of those lying at rest when he took this late 50s shot across All Saints Square from a position in the churchyard. In the distance we can see Woolworth's store on Effingham Street, below the Old College Inn on the corner with College Street. The mock Tudor building on the left belonged to George Schonhut, the beef and pork butcher. Gladly, we still have individual shops like this today, even if the supermarkets have driven so many proprietors to the wall. How much more satisfying and reliable it is to have someone who knows about meat. A proper butcher makes his own tasty sausages, minces his own beef and is not averse to throwing in a few scraps for Fido to enjoy. When was the last time you bought a lamb shank from the supermarket meat counter and felt that the lad with acne, who two minutes ago was selling lottery tickets, actually knew his rump steak from his elbow? Next door to Schonhut's was the 'window to watch', as adverts for John Collier's tailoring preached. Remember the Rael-Brook poplin shirts sold here, once over, that danced on the washing line during the commercial break on ITV? You did not have to iron them, or so we were promised.

Below: The end of the line for trams in Rotherham came in 1949 and it was none too soon for this car, as evidenced by its battle-scarred exterior displayed as it took the Howard Street/Effingham Street corner. The powers that be probably thought that it was just throwing good money down the drain to effect any form of cosmetic surgery on the old warhorse that was only a few months away from the knackers' yard. Even though a few more bumps and scrapes would not have made much difference, the conductor was taking matters seriously. He had disembarked so that he could watch the tram's progress past the parked car on the left that had been abandoned by a thoughtless driver. Hands on hips, the conductor muttered to himself about the stupidity of others. The tram operator had a difficult job negotiating his vehicle along the tracks as it was a single ended car that needed to be reversed along Effingham Street to the terminus. Two imposing buildings overlooked the corner. The Town Hall Chambers, on the right, included Alfred Alcock's wholesale electrical shop. Across from here, the ostentatiously titled British and Colonial Footwear Company did business underneath an advert for Wolf power tools. In the distance the Gas Works chimney on Frederick Street belched out its pall of smoke that grubbied even the best Omo-white shirts.

Above: The trolleybus in the distance is about to approach the photographer and use the turning circle where he was standing, before joining the queue of buses on the left. It will pass two other vehicles that can be seen rivalling one another on Effingham Street in the late 1950s. A Morris Minor makes its way past the bus waiting to set off on the Broom Valley route. On the other side of the road a parked Volkswagen sits outside Cantors, the house furnishers. These two cars vied for popularity as the cost of motoring came within the reach of ordinary families. Under the Macmillan government we entered a phase in our economy that the prime minister, or 'Supermac' as cartoonists dubbed him, referred to as 'the never had it so good' period. High employment and cheaper goods made it a welcome change from the austerity of the immediate postwar years. Alec Issigonis (1906-88), the son of a Greek merchant, was born in Turkey but emigrated to Britain in 1922 as a teenager. He soon adopted this land as his new home and very quickly became one of us. He joined Morris Motors in 1936 as a suspension designer and developed the Morris Minor, which remained in production from 1948 to 1971. It was the first all-British car to pass the 1,000,000 mark in sales and surviving models are still cherished by owners and collectors. In 1959 he introduced the Mini, another major rival to the VW Beetle. The German car, one of the few foreign vehicles on our roads in those days, was the brainchild of Ferdinand Porsche (1875-1951). He designed his first 'people's car' in 1934 and went on to develop the Tiger tank for the German army in World War II.

Top right: High Street was a much brighter and busier part of town on 15 May 1965 than it is today.

Leading the way on opposite pavements were two young women who represented the youthful trend in shorter skirt lengths. Before long they would have gone the whole hog and not just bared a knee, but displayed much of a thigh as well. Mary Quant, the doyenne of mid-60s modern fashion design, opened her first boutique, 'Bazaar', in Chelsea in 1964. By the end of the following year hemlines had risen, along with mum's eyebrows and dad's blood pressure. The model, Jean Shrimpton, was banned from a racecourse in Melbourne for wearing a mini-skirt and economists scratched their heads in working out how to classify the new dresses. Children's clothing was exempt from purchase tax and minis were often sold as items for girls, rather than adults, to keep down the price. Dry cleaners even started to charge by the inch, rather than per piece! High Street still had its cobbles and old tramlines in the mid-60s, even though the boneshakers had stopped running more than 15 years earlier. The 'No Waiting' sign outside the Old Bank Buildings is a reminder that the street had to be kept clear as it was still part of the main A630 road to Sheffield.

Far right: Looking down Corporation Street towards Chantry Bridge on 15 May 1965, the Odeon Cinema can be seen on the left. It opened as the Regal on 22 December 1934, with Sandy Powell in attendance. That fine comic, with his 'Can you hear me, mother?' catchphrase, was certain to have helped swell the first day crowds. The very first film to be shown was 'Girls

please'. Sandy is reputed to have said, 'I bet they do', though that was a little risqué for him. The movie was a farce by Sydney Howard, the Yorkshire comedian. Prominent amongst the entertainment offered in those early days were organ interludes, featuring that wizard of the pipes, stops and bellows, Thomas Dando. Going to the pictures, as we called it, became a regular weekly occurrence. Audiences boomed during the 30s, 40s and well into the 50s before television and bingo came to call. The Regal was leased to the Odeon Circuit during the war and renamed later as part of the chain originally developed by Oscar Deutsch (1893-1941). Plans were submitted in August 1962 to turn the café into a ballroom for the Victor Sylvester School of Dancing, about the same time as the cinema seating capacity was reduced by 500. Rank Leisure took over the administration and applied for a bingo licence in 1974, much to the disgust of the Borough Chairman. These plans were dropped and Rank gave up the lease the following year, to be succeeded by Twainville Ltd who renamed it as the Scala.

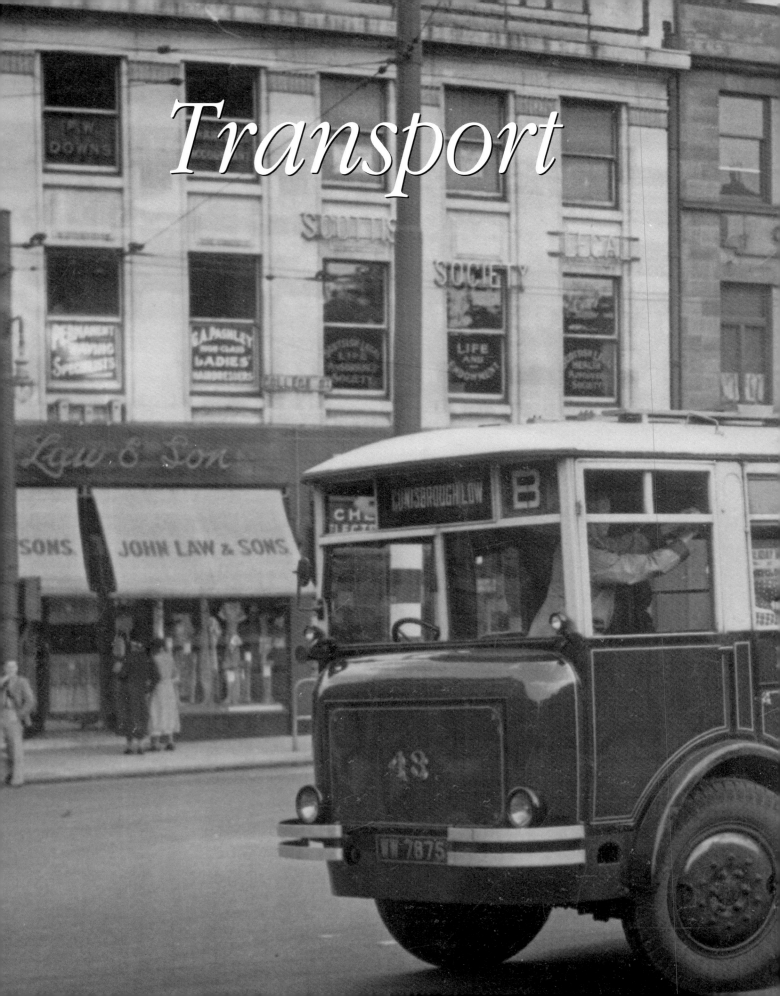

Transport

Off to Conisbrough Low in the 1930s, perhaps to visit the Norman castle that helped to inspire Sir Walter Scott to write 'Ivanhoe', these passengers boarded the Garrett that displayed the red and cream livery of the Mexborough and Swinton Traction Company. The colour scheme was to change to green and cream after the war. The M and S company used letters to name its routes, whereas Rotherham deployed the more traditional number system. Consequently, the trip to the castle could be by route B or 25, whichever took your fancy! Was this a case of individuality or sheer bloody-mindedness? We will leave the reader to draw a conclusion. Behind the bus, across the road, we can make out a branch of Grafton's, the family baker that is still in business today elsewhere in Rotherham. Horace Brook, the florist and fruiterer, also traded in this vicinity. Fresh fruit from a specialist shop was an interesting phenomenon. Today, our shops and supermarkets can provide perishable goods all the year round, thanks to fridges, freezers and imports. But, there was a time when the seasons of the year often determined the produce that was available. Strawberries were available in June, to be followed by raspberries. Apples were there during the summer, but our winter months left us relying on what could be safely stored or brought in by the banana boats. The only peaches you could have in December were sliced up and eaten from tins.

Above: The well respected jeweller, Francis Lowe, appeared to be asking for help by sending out an SOS on his shop sign. However, it was just a case of an errant letter, rather than any grave misfortune that had come to trouble the purveyor of a variety of pretty and ornamental items that ranged from rings and crystal to prize cups. The shutters had been pulled down on the business in this late 1940s photograph. Notice the fashion of the quartet walking past the single decker 'trackless', as Rotherham folk liked to call their trolleybuses, that was bound for the delightfully named Worry Goose Lane. The man was probably wearing his demob suit, provided for use in civvy street after so many years in uniform serving in the armed forces during World War II. His attractive companions, with their mid calf skirts, sported modern hairstyles not dissimilar from those favoured by the popular singing trio from across the Atlantic, the Andrews Sisters. Perhaps these ladies were off to find an apple tree under which they could sit with their companion, especially if he had been a bugle boy in Company B. Looking further down Effingham Street, the quartet was heading towards the old Rotherham Advertiser offices. This street's name reminds us of the 3rd Earl of Effingham who passionately objected to British colonial policy in 18th century America. There is even a city in east Illinois named for him.

Below: Traffic is now banned from this spot since the pedestrianisation of most of Effingham Street and Henry Street, to the right. The road behind the double decker Daimler trolley now leads towards the inner bypass where it becomes an entry slip road and flyover. The conglomeration of overhead cabling illustrates that this was where the trolleybuses had a turning circle, though by July 1963 only those servicing Brecks and Wickersley were in operation as the Maltby route had been given over to motorbuses in 1954. Effingham Street was constructed in the 1850s as part of the development carried out by the Earl of Effingham, Lord of the Manor of Rotherham. The imposing Advertiser offices, from where the local paper published its mixture of news and notices of hatches, matches and dispatches, were demolished in 1986 and a new Boot's building erected the following year. Henry Garnett's printing and publishing company was based in this old building from the early 1930s until just before its demise, moving its works to Eastwood in 1984. The first structure on this site was erected in 1860 by the Wesleyan Reform Church as a Zion Chapel. It had room for a congregation of 600, a reflection of the religious commitment of our Victorian forefathers. In 1911 the chapel was converted, not in a religious sense, but in terms of usage, into a cinema. It became the Electric Pavilion, later the Electra Picture Palace.

Centre: Rotherham showed an interest in trolleybus operation long before many similar English towns. As early as 1910, the Corporation sent a working party to study systems being set up on the continent. Soon, the first examples of this revolutionary form of public transport were in place, initially as feeders to the tram network that had been inaugurated in 1903. Three single deckers, built by David Brown for the Railless Electric Traction Company, went into service as Corporation trolleybuses on 3 October 1912 from the Stag Inn on Herringthorpe Lane to Maltby, passing through Bramley and Wickersley on the way. Trolleybuses lasted until 2 October 1965, providing a service to the community for exactly 53 years. If only the passengers on this service had appreciated the value of memorabilia they might have hung on to their bus tickets. Some of the special ones have become collectors' items. It is amazing how such simple items can have a value, but 'trackless' buffs are always on the lookout for a piece of the golden years of Rotherham public transport. While they may not be worth as much as a first day cover penny black stamp, tickets from that final trolleybus journey on the Kimberworth to Thrybergh route are worth more than a few bob.

Bottom: Corporation Street by the middle of the 1960s was awash with traffic. The rise in private car ownership meant that Britain's towns and cities had to begin to adopt measures that would avoid a complete snarl up on roads never meant to accommodate such a volume. Large car parks, no waiting areas, box junctions, one way systems and bypasses were created in an effort to keep the roads from turning into a series of logjams. Pedestrianised areas were developed to encourage shoppers to use town centre retail outlets, but this just threw more pressure onto the feeder streets. It is a problem that has yet to be solved, 40 years on. Pity the poor learner driver on the left, attempting to weave a path past stationary vehicles while keeping an eye on the vans, cars and buses all around him. If all his practice had taken place here he would never have got out of first gear. His vehicle would shortly pass the Odeon cinema, on the left. This would become the Scala in 1975 and, after refurbishment, be turned into the Ritz Bingo Club in 1989. Clients interested in legs eleven or two fat ladies were able to enjoy a trip down memory lane in between games. The Conacher organ was restored to working order and was played during the interval, evoking reminiscences of the great days in the 1930s when a number of radio broadcasts were made from here. Then, the organist really did pull out all the stops.

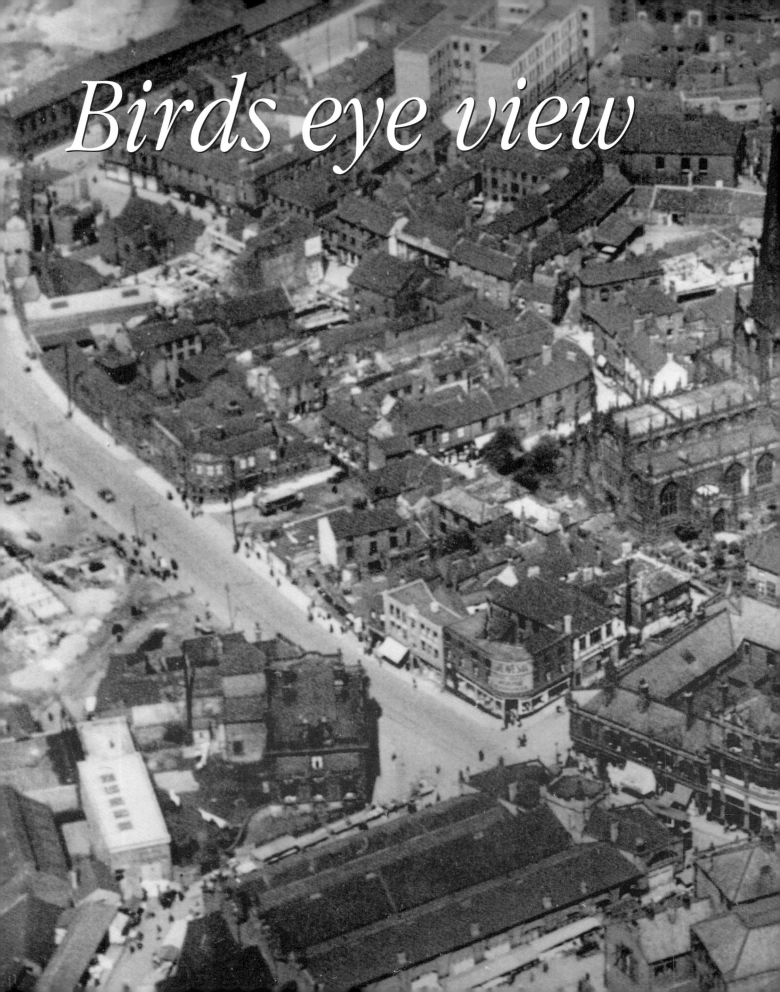

Birds eye view

It was only in the first decade of the 20th century that the Wright brothers got off the ground at Kitty Hawk to open up the skies for us all. Within a few short years, Blériot had flown the Channel and Baron von Richtofen was doing battle with the Royal Flying Corps in his red Fokker triplane during the first world war. So rapidly did aircraft technology advance that Alcock and Brown achieved the first Atlantic air crossing as early as 1919. Inspired by such developments, during the 1920s aerial reconnaissance became part of peacetime activity designed to help map our settlements and countryside. Town planners drew on photographs like this one to enhance their appreciation of the current layout of streets and buildings. The pilot taking this shot was obviously active in this era as the buildings we can see above the parish church were demolished by 1930 to make way for the creation of All Saints Square. The parish church in the centre, topped by its 180 foot spire, has connections with the monks of Rufford Abbey who rebuilt the earlier church over a 200-year period up to the 15th century. It was restored in 1873-75 by Gilbert Scott. Other notable landmarks include Mason's, to the right and below the church, at the top of High Street, noticeable for a series of shop awnings. Market Hall is at the bottom left, with Corporation Street snaking away from here towards the top of the picture.

Taken over 75 years ago, this view of Rotherham is a mixture of the recognisable and the unfamiliar to anyone under 40. Sharp-eyed observers should just make out the top of All Saints' spire at the bottom of the photograph. From this fixed point we can get our bearings. The buildings at the bottom left were replaced by All Saints Square in the early 1930s. From here, Effingham Street runs diagonally left to cross Howard Street and meet with Henry Street to the right of the building that was then occupied by Garnett's, the printer of the Rotherham Advertiser. The old Hippodrome stands to the right of Garnett's, on the

Howard Street corner, while further along Howard Street, where Centenary Market is now located, the Royal Picture House attracted a healthy custom in those days. It began life at the start of 1894 as the Theatre Royal and, after several makeovers, closed in 1957 as the Regent when it had been reduced to staging second-rate bills that included striptease artistes such as Phyllis Dixey. Continuing right, Howard Street joins High Street, seen coming up from the bottom. College Street and Percy Street also meet High Street from the left as it heads off towards Doncaster Gate by the Moorish design of the Cinema House building.

Working life

Work in the foundries and rolling mills was hard work. It was a tough life that demanded similarly tough men who had themselves been forged at home rather than nurtured. But they were more than just traditional examples of masculinity because they had skills honed to perfection on the shop floor. Years of experience were deployed at Ickles in the early 1930s when using a double-acting steam hammer to forge axles too small in quantity for the continuous processes in the axle hammer shop. Armature shafts, small rolls, shafting and miscellaneous engineering forgings between a quarter ton and two tons were produced here. Material to be forged was heated in a coal-fired continuous furnace or in one of two batch type coal-fired furnaces. This group of workmen was using a five ton axle hammer. Iron smelting and steel production have long been associated with Rotherham. Evidence of iron working has been discovered at Templeborough that dates back to Roman times. Allied to a large output from the coalfields in the 19th century, iron and steel provided much of the town's wealth at that time, building upon the enterprise of the Walker family which established a foundry in 1754 where Rotherham Forge and Rolling Mill was later to stand.

Half a dozen baby-boomers, as children born in the immediate postwar era came to be known, were being bounced on knees in Cranworth Road clinic in 1946. When men returned to their wives and sweethearts after years away at the battlefront or locked up in prison camps, it was not surprising that couples did what came naturally. Anyone with shares in nappies or Farley's rusks made a fortune. The birth rate soared and mums and their offspring descended on the clinics for advice and health checks. Britons were quite fit. That was largely accidental as it was determined for them by a diet strong on vegetables and low in fats and meat products because of wartime rationing. This clinic was obviously keen on the mantra of fresh air and exercise, as illustrated by the slogan on the wall. 'Sun and air and water pure, we can't keep well without. So fling your windows open wide and drive the microbes out.' Those of us who came into the world at that time had mothers who seemed obsessed with cleanliness. We could not touch anything that was a little dirty 'because you might catch germs' and we always had to wash behind our ears. We never did discover what evils lurked there, but obeyed like good boys and girls.

Above: The rapid rise of the railways as an influential force on our way of life began with those trials at Rainhill in 1829 when Stephenson's 'Rocket' demonstrated its ability to provide the pulling power for a trainload of passengers. The goods line from Stockton to Darlington had been inaugurated four years earlier, but it was the movement of people that changed family life forever. For generations, we had lived, worked and died in the same neck of the woods as our forefathers. Yet, within some 30 years of the birth of first passenger rail service whole families had decamped from their home territory and moved to the four corners of the country. Rotherham saw its first puff of steam from a locomotive stack in 1838. The Sheffield and Rotherham Railway Company established a line along the Don Valley from the Wicker in Sheffield to Westgate Station, Rotherham's very first. The North Midland Railway Company developed a vaguely parallel line from Derby to Masbrough and Leeds that opened in 1840. These companies later became part of Midland Railway. Westgate Station closed on 4 October 1952 when Mayor W Young did the honours and waved goodbye to locomotive 40409 and a piece of history. Rotherham's Central Station is now located off College Road.

Right: Clocking on, just in time for the two-ten shift. Workers put their cards into the machine, pressed the handle and put their time stamped cards onto the rack where they stayed until they repeated the process by clocking out. They went through this routine every day of their working lives at the Steel, Peech and Tozer plant at Templeborough. The young man, second in the queue, was obviously careful about his appearance. His hair was slicked back with Brylcreem, still popular even at the start of the 1960s. The older men favoured the traditional short back and sides look that required little more than a quick scratch every morning as a form of grooming. The works were built on lands that were once owned by the Abbot of Roche. They stayed in the monastery hands form the 13th century until dissolution in 1538. The monks are thought to have operated mills, but nothing like the great steel mills that were developed during the industrial revolution. Steel production in the area started in 1833 and Hampton and Radcliffe installed a manufacturing plant in 1871, though the property was taken over by the Phoenix Bessemer Steel Company the following year. When this enterprise went bust in 1875, the appropriately named Henry Steel formed a new company as Steel, Tozer and Hampton. After Hampton left in 1883, William Peech's name came to the fore to give the company its famous title.

Oh the joys of school assembly. Every day began with the taking of the register in the classroom and the monitor for the week putting the straws into milk bottles sitting in the crate that the caretaker had brought round earlier in the morning. Once our dinner money had been handed in, Sir took us down to the hall in a long crocodile. We waited in silence and stood when the headmaster came in and waited for the teacher at the piano to play the introduction to 'There is a green hill far away'. Brinsworth Junior School must have been quite a progressive establishment in 1956 because some of the children are sitting on the floor. A girl reads a prayer from the lectern under the watchful gaze of 'the boss'. That was quite novel, too, because the head usually dominated the proceedings. He was in charge of everything during assembly. Each one followed a similar pattern with songs, prayers and a moral lecture illustrated by a story from the Bible or about the life of Helen Keller. Then there would be congratulations for the football team winning its last match and a public telling off for any precocious eight year-old who wanted to go to the toilet. Then it was back to class where we started our working day with a mental arithmetic test.

Any old iron

Remember the rag and bone man with his horse and cart and his cry of 'Any old iron?' Things have moved on a lot since those now long gone days. Dealing in scrap metal today is a highly skilled job - and not a goldfish or balloon in sight.

For more than three decades the Rotherham firm of Special Alloys (Northern) Ltd located in Greasborough Road has been a name to be reckoned with in the field of Specialised metal recycling.

The firm was started in 1971 by Brian Ackroyd, Victor Jacques and Brian Stacey. The trio had met at the firm of Thomas W Ward where they had each started work after leaving school. Soon afterwards they went their separate ways but met up again in 1966 when all three found themselves working at JR Fairclough in Brinsworth: putting their heads and money together they decided to go on their own.

The new business started from a temporary building in Fullerton Road from where they bought and sold metals. Some 18 months later they moved to their present base where the team would eventually grow to 15 staff including their new Specialised engineering company SA Flanges Ltd., and from one industrial unit to the three at Greasbrough Road plus the engineering works on Thornhill

Victor Jacques' son Nick joined the firm in 1975; Brian Ackroyd's son, another Nick, joined in 1978: today both are joint managing directors of the company.

By the time the two Nicks had arrived on the scene the firm had already begun expanding the business.

Today sales of alloy scraps are based on very careful inspection, segregation and processing of both 'guaranteed' as well as mixed parcels of materials.

In the hi-tech modern world materials are made available for segregation by spark testing, spectrographic checking and wet analysis. After sorting, metals are de-greased, shot blasted and packed ready for despatch.

Attention to detail and quality control have gained the firm national recognition and approvals to supply leading Aerospace Manufacturers.

The scrap metal business has certainly come a long way since the days of 'Any old iron.'

Top: Founders (L-R) Mr V Jacques, Mr B V Stacey and Mr B Ackroyd. **Bottom left:** *An early company vehicle.* **Left:** *A view inside the works.* **Bottom:** *A birds eye view of Special Alloys (Northern) Ltd, Greasborough Road,*

Life long learning

'Education, education, education' is the often repeated mantra of politicians; but education is far more just than a 21st century political slogan. Like many of today's further education colleges Rotherham College - the Rotherham College of Arts and Technology to give it its full title - traces its origins to a 19th Mechanics Institute.

In an era of education for all it is difficult to comprehend just how great was the thirst for knowledge and self improvement amongst the working classes in late Victorian times. Many of those who attended evening classes were the first generation of their families who had been able to read and write. Anyone who looks

Top: *The Howard Building in the 1930s.*
Right: *The library in the Howard Building.*
Below: *Students learn the art of silversmithing.*

through the marriage registers of say the 1850s will quickly see that many of those who had just taken their marriage vows would sign the register only with an X.

But that situation was set to change with a number of Education Acts which provided for at last a minimum of education for everyone. Children may still have left school at 12, or even younger, to work in the mining industry and factories, but by then they had at least mastered the minimum skills, reading, writing and arithmetic, necessary to permit them to aspire to greater things.

Working folk who had lived in the shadow of ignorance and who had to rely on their betters to read and write letters for them and to tell them what

was going on in the world, could now read it for themselves in newspapers whose sales were surging in the face of the new mass market for printed material.

Though the primary education offered to everyone may have been rudimentary it provided the minimum tools necessary to better oneself, and created a demand for even more precious knowledge. In an age when further education was a rare commodity it was sought after and valued to a degree which is almost inconceivable today. And not just for its own sake: knowledge, as we know, is power.

Trades Unions were well aware of the value of education and that its acquisition would allow working men to deal as equals with employers and the upper classes who managed and owned businesses and who governed the country. For this reason if no other social-ists of all hues supported and encouraged further education, quite as much as those business leaders who for reasons of their own wanted a well educated workforce. Mechanics Intitites would be the vehicles through which working men, and women, would for the first time in history be able to obtain a level of education which until then had been almost exclusively restricted to their 'betters'.

The facade of the Rotherham and Masborough Literary and Mechanics Institute still stands at the corner of Effingham Street and Howard Street as part of the old Town Hall development. The Institute was built in 1853 and became the home of the first School of Science and Art. There were also several other small institutes based around the town until the building of the College of Technology in Howard Street.

At the time of its opening in 1931 by the Right Hon. Lord Aberconway many residents regarded the new College as being too large, and pessimistically predicted that it would be something of a white elephant which would never be fully utilised.

The staff at the time the College opened comprised a Principal and five full-time staff with a number of part-time lecturers. Courses for 'seniors' included mechanical and electrical engineering, mining, metallurgy, car maintenance, welding and joinery. There were also courses in what was then referred to in the College prospectus as 'women's work': needlework, cookery, dressmaking and laundry. It was also possible to study for external degrees of the

Top: Students in the Science lab.
Above: A needlework lesson in the 1930s.

London University in Mechanical and Electrical Engineering and Science.

Students in those now far off times found conditions somewhat different than today. The College prospectus in the early 1930s contained a stern warning: 'students are forbidden to loiter on the College steps or in the precinct entrances'. Modes of transport to the College too were also rather different than today. Transport privilege tickets were available to enable students to get half fares on buses and trams. Students who spurned public transport in favour of making their own arrangements for travel were warned 'No bicycles may be taken inside the College - a shed for storage is provided'.

As a reflection of the close links with local industry the College launched an Engineering Society in the early 1930s with prominent local industrialists amongst its members. The Society would continue organising lectures, film and slide shows and visits for its members well into the 1970s.

Despite the doomsayers of 1931 by 1942 the College had developed sufficiently to organise its activities into a number of departments each of which published its own prospectus. There were departments of Mining, Mechanical and Civil Engineering and Building, Electrical Engineering, Physics and Maths, and Commerce and Administration. For nearly 40 years these same areas would continue to reflect the

Top and Right: Students getting to grips with the craft of cabinet making. Above: HRH the Duke of Edinburgh chats to a student on his visit to open the Clifton Building as an extension to the College.

College's links with training and education to suit the needs of the local economy and the wider community.

During the second World War, despite the inevitable dislocation caused by many staff and students being called up to serve in the forces, the College of Technology continued to provide courses. A local Rotherham man, Peter Disbe, was based at the College in 1943 after he joined the RAF. Whilst waiting to be called to active service anyone who did not possess a school certificate was expected to study for a Certificate of General Education. Servicemen travelled from all parts of the country to Rotherham to go through a six month course at the College. Mr Disbe came up from London at the age of 18 to join the course and would later recall 'the people of Rotherham were very good to us; we were welcomed and very much spoilt by their generosity'.

Meanwhile the notes of the meetings of the staff union in the 1940s give some indication of the wartime activities at the College. Staff were expected to take their turn in the evenings and at night on fire-watching duties; a position on the roof of the College provided a good look out point for enemy bombs dropping on Rotherham, not to mention any incendiaries dropping on the roof of the College itself.

Following the war the College began to offer full-time courses, which occupied about 30 hours a week. A Student Association was established with the Principal as its president, with the aim 'to increase the social and recreational activities of the students'. In addition to the Engineering Society a Society for Administrative Studies was now established; this was attended by local people who wanted 'an interchange of experience in supervision'. For an annual subscription of five shillings (25p) it provided local managers with an opportunity to discuss the problems of 'supervision'.

The School of Arts and Crafts was housed on the top floor of the College with a Headmaster and 13 staff. It offered courses in cabinet-making, silversmithing, bookbinding and weaving in addition to ceramics, painting and drawing.

By 1950 the College was employing over 60 full-time staff teaching and support staff, and over 100 visiting lecturers. A number of scholarships were available to prospective students, and achievement was obviously

much valued. In 1952 a notice of the Prize Day pointed out that 'accommodation is strictly limited; parents and others desiring tickets of admission should make an early application to the Principal'. A contemporary photograph of the College Hall (now the College Keynote Delivery Suite in the Howard Building) shows a splendid oak-panelled room with serried ranks of sturdy oak chairs laid out in front of a formal stage.

Official attitudes to smoking reflected a strong sense of pragmatism about the students of the day; even so the following notice must have been thought curiously discriminatory to those who read it in the 1950s: 'Smoking is strictly forbidden in College except in the Mining Department and in certain laboratories with the permission of the appropriate Head of Department'.

In 1959 the College became the subject of national newspaper headlines, but not, unhappily, because of any academic achievements. On 7th April 1959, inside the College's General office (now the Howard reception area), a physics lecturer, Bernard Walden, took his revenge on a young secretary, Joyce Moran, who had spurned his proposal of marriage by shooting her dead with a Luger pistol. In the foyer of the College (now the Howard Building) he also shot a former student, Neil Saxton, who was his rival for Miss Moran's affections. Neil Saxton later died in hospital of his injuries. Bernard Walden fled to Leeds where he was eventually arrested. Tried at Sheffield assizes Walden was later hanged at Armley Prison in Leeds on 14th August 1959; he was one of the last people to be executed in England.

In a happier vein, by the late 1950s the single building was proving too small to cope with the demands made upon it and plans for expansion were being made. On 2nd September 1961 the Clifton Building was opened as an extension to the College by HRH the Duke of Edinburgh. Now the College offered GCE O levels and A levels, ONCs, ONDs and HNCs in a wide variety of disciplines. Mining courses were well supported by the local coal industry, and there were opportunities for students to work their way up from 'entrants training' to degree-equivalent qualifications. The College now had a Department of Maths and 'women's work' had become the notably less sexist Department of Household Management and Technology. There were also new College annexes at Brinsworth Street and Doncaster Gate next door to the Civic Theatre.

The College prospectus for the early 1960s also began offering a Meat Traders Course with a timetable which included English, Geography, Arithmetic, Scientific Principles and Meat Inspection as well as a 'Quicker Reading' a short course for executives.

The driving force behind the further education expansion programme of the 1960s was the 1964 Industrial Training Act which arose from a belief that the traditional apprenticeship of serving one's time making tea and running errands was no longer working, not least because an increasing emphasis on piecework meant fewer tradesmen had the time to train youngsters.

The new Act set up some 17 Industrial Training Boards, of which those of the Coal industry and the Engineering industry would have some of the most influence at Rotherham College. The new courses were funded by financial levies imposed by the Boards on their respective industries - and in turn those industries could employ those apprentices with no additional educational cost.

In the early 1970s the College acquired old school premises to establish a Building annexe on Park street and a Foundry annexe on Clough Road.

Meanwhile, in 1970, the School of Arts had became the Rotherham College of Arts and Community Studies. In 1980 a new building, now the Eastwood Building, was built to house this new college. In 1981 Rotherham Council made the decision to combine the two neighbouring colleges, and Rotherham College of Arts and Technology, RCAT, came into being.

The 1980s saw a rapid decline in the local mining and steel industries and a consequent decline in demand for related courses within the College. Adapting to meet these changes in the local economy the College developed and expanded its courses in social care, business and management, computer skills, hairdressing and catering. There was also a growth in courses aimed specifically at the unemployed, including opportunities within community sites which the College operated.

Today RCAT is still a premier provider of education, serving the educational needs of Rotherham's communities. The vast portfolio of full and part-time courses that the College offers means that people have unprecedented opportunities for a lifetime of learning.

The College has come a vast distance from its early days in the 1930s, and it is continually evolving. March 1st 2004 marked another historic day for the College when RCAT and the Rotherham Managing Agency (RMA), the work-based learning provider, merged to form a single entity. The development will in future allow the merged organisation to improve its services bringing in its wake new and exciting opportunities for employees and trainees alike.

RCAT has become an integral part of Rotherham life through the diverse opportunities for learning which the College has provided down the decades. The College with its outreach programmes in the community and its strong links with Sheffield Hallam University, together with its extensive portfolio continues to offer endless educational opportunities for everyone.

Far left and below: *The Clifton and Eastwood Buildings pictured in 2004.*

Rocks and rolling

The names of Ben Bennett Jr Ltd and the Eastwood Rolling Mills have been familiar to local folk for generations past. But how many readers we wonder can recall who Ben Bennett junior was, let alone recall Ben Bennett senior?

The firm of Ben Bennett Jr Ltd has its origins in Rotherham in the second half of the 19th century, and became a limited company in the 1920s. Today the business is split into two divisions: Eastwood Rolling Mills established in the 1930s, and Grange Mill Quarry, also acquired prior to the second world war; there is also a thriving transport department.

Eastwood Rolling Mills located in Rotherham specialises in the manufacture of mild, carbon and hardened and tempered steel strip mainly for clutch material, knife blades, springs and general presswork applications. Up to 10 per cent of the rolling mill's output is exported. Grange Mill Quarry is located near Matlock in Derbyshire and specialises in the production of high purity limestone in both lump stone and as finely graded powders. The bulk of the limestone is for industrial applications such as glass-making, pharmaceuticals and rubber compounds.

Since 1938 the company's head office has been based at Danecourt in Lisle Road, the firm having moved there from Whiston Grange and even earlier from an office at the top of Hollowgate. The business' very first office however was merely a room above a sweet shop at the bottom of Doncaster Gate.

The founder of the Bennett family was John Bennett a blacksmith chain maker and a giant of a man, weighing 20 stone and six feet tall, who in 1861 moved to this area from Dudley in the Midlands.

In 1883 at the age of 23 John Bennett's son, an engineer, Ben Bennett, went into business as a mill furnisher in Rotherham on his own account and soon prospered with the growth of industry in South Yorkshire occurring at that time.

Ben's son, a second Ben Bennett, was born in 1889, and in due course entered the family business.

After serving in the Army from the start of the Great War, and being invalided out 18 months later with rheumatic fever, Ben junior developed his own business supplying of scrap iron and steel to the steel industry around Rotherham and Sheffield. The elder Ben Bennett died in 1925, just before his and his son's businesses combined to become a private limited company: a timing which resulted in the unusual 'Jr.' appearing in the company name.

The following year the general strike led to a shortage of coal. Ever resourceful the still youthful Ben Bennett bought a drift mine near Barnsley which he named the Little Barbara Mine after his eldest daughter; he kept

Top: *Founder of the company John Bennett and his wife Hannah.* **Below left and below:** *The original Ben Bennett and pictured below his wife Lillian, son Ben and daughter Poppy.*

the mine going for over a year until the coal shortage resolved itself. Though the mine soon closed the exercise would lead to an interest in quarrying which would have important long term consequences for the company.

In 1933 Ben Bennett junior began quarrying basalt at Taddington near Buxton, soon a considerable business was built up in dry tarred and bituminous road stone. This new venture was to be incorporated as another private company under the name of Hardmac Ltd.

During 1935 Ben Bennett joined with others in an undertaking known as Associated Quartzites Ltd a jointly owned company formed to produce sand and quartzite chippings for the building industry and for roadstone from mineral deposits at Blaxton not far from Doncaster. Also in 1935 Ben the second acquired his first interest in the limestone industry when yet another company, Super Limes Ltd, was incorporated to quarry limestone at Grange Mill in Derbyshire.

Ben Bennett had spent nearly all his life in the great steel producing area of Rotherham and Sheffield and in 1936 he acquired land next to the Eastwood trading estate in Rotherham where he built the Eastwood Rolling Mills to carry out the manufacture of cold rolled strip steel.

A former employee of Habershons, Joe Uttley, supplied the technical know how and sales ability necessary to go into the cold rolled steel business. Ben Bennett provided the capital. At the time in the 'Hungry Thirties' nearly all the other steel owners in the area

were either heavily in debt or closing down. And in fact Ben Bennett would never live to see a penny profit from the investment. Just before the second world war began an offer was made to buy the plant by a rival firm; in the circumstances it was an offer that many would have accepted.

Ultimately all the various Bennett undertakings, including the rolling mill would flourish, though many difficulties would have to be overcome. In the meantime Ben's three daughters Barbara, Joan and Mary together with his son Ben Bennett the Third all entered the family business in their turn.

The third Ben Bennett's entry to the family firm was not however without its hiccups. Having fallen in love with a junior secretary in the head office young Ben's father sacked both his son and the secretary. Happily the two young lovers would be reconciled with the elder Ben, and their marriage would be a long one, lasting until the younger Ben's death in 1989.

Back in the 1930s however, the lovestruck, and now redundant, son found work as an electrician's mate for a Sheffield company, but with the second world war imminent he joined the regular army as a member of the Yorks and Lancs Artillery Regiment and was initially employed firing Bofors guns defending Britain's cities from air raids. Two years later it was discovered that Ben had been a public schoolboy, and as a result he was recommended

Top left: *A family photograph circa 1919.*
Top right, both pictures: *Ben Bennett Jr (who the company is named after) and his wife Georgina.*
Above: *Ben and Georgina Bennett's daughters Joan (left), Mary (right) and Barbara (centre).*

for commissioning as an officer. Ben refused the offer, being more than proud enough of his rank as sergeant. Now Ben was transferred to the Dorset Regiment and was shipped out to Burma to fight the Japanese, staying in the Far East until 1946.

The senior Ben Bennett had died in 1939 at the age of just 50 after an eventful and strenuous life. At the time of his death his son had having already been a member of the Territorial Army had already joined up in anticipation of the outbreak of war with Germany. During the war it therefore fell to the eldest of the Bennett girls, Barbara Bennett, to assume the responsibilities of Chairman and Managing Director of the company through the arduous and difficult years of the conflict.

Miss Bennett was ably supported by the other members of the Board but late in 1940 she was compelled to resign some of her duties due to ill health. During the remainder of the war the Board of Directors would be headed by Charles W Cooper, a son-in law of Ben Bennett II's, and FJ Kershaw.

The outbreak of war should have been the signal for the firm to move into profit with a massive increase in demand for steel. Things were however rather more complicated. The government decided it was not going to tolerate the kind of unwholesome profiteering which had occurred during the first world war and brought out its Excess Profits Tax based on average earnings in the last three years of peace; given that the rolling mill had been making no profits at all this was a problem - though fortuitously one which would balance itself out when the previously highly profitably quarrying side of the business now recorded losses. Before the war however, the only hardening and tempering steel had been imported from Sweden but by 1940 that supply had come to an end. The government now approached firms such as Bennett's and asked them to install

Top left: Ben Bennett III. *Top right: Whiston Grange, Ben Bennett's third head office.* **Left:** *Built by Ben Bennett Jr. Dane Court was to become the company's fourth head office and is still used today.*

hardening and tempering furnaces with the Government paying the cost. However, rather than being subsidised by the Government Bennett's paid for their own new equipment using cash from the sale of a quarry at Calton Hill.

In 1946 the company bought Furness Quarry at Stoney Middleton Dale in Derbyshire a purchase which coincided with the return from the war of Ben Bennett the third. He now devoted himself to modernising and mechanising the newly acquired quarry, and within a few years this was producing large quantities of finely ground limestone and limestone chippings.

During 1952 Ben Bennett was formally appointed Chairman and Managing Director. At the same time the company Board of Directors was reconstituted as a purely family affair, made up of just Ben Bennett and his three sisters with the managers of the several departments appointed as 'Special Directors'.

After the war years considerable sums were spent in installing modern plant and machinery at the company's quarries and its steel mill to keep abreast of rapidly changing demands of industry, and in particular the mechanisation of road and airfield construction.

The products of the limestone quarries by now included hard Derbyshire limestone chippings and finely ground limestone in all commercial grades, materials which were supplied to manufacturers, contractors and builders as far north as Glasgow and as far south as Cornwall - a nation-wide demand which was a reflection of the remarkable properties of the limestone beds and the consistent grading of the products. At the time the demand for those products seemed to continually increase.

As for steel, by the late 1950s the Eastwood Rolling Mills had expanded considerably and was by now manufacturing hardened and tempered spring steel strip in addition to bright cold rolled steel strip in all qualities.

During the post war years of 1946 to 1976 more than three quarters of the profits would be ploughed back into the business. By 1966 however, the Furness Quarry was producing 20,000 tons per month but was capable of producing double that figure if sufficient money could be raised to fund new equipment. Unknown to Bennett's another

Top: *Eastwood Rolling Mills, 1957.*
Right: *A Staff Dinner Dance in the 1960s.*

company's quarry, Derbyshire Stone's Matlock quarry, was running out of stone and an approach was made by Derbyshire Stone to buy out Bennett's Furness Quarry - an offer which was accepted enabling the money which would have been spent on new quarry plant to be spent elsewhere.

The proceeds of the quarry sale enabled Bennett's to modernise the Eastwood Rolling Mills and to mechanise its Grange Mill quarry - as well as transforming the company's fleet of lorries into a tanker fleet. A further rationalisation of business interests around this time also saw the sale of the shareholding in Associated Quartzite and the disposal

of the company's scrap metal interests. Consolidation of business interests became the overall objective.

Meanwhile yet another Ben Bennett had been born in 1941; he would join the company in 1958, marrying his wife Norma in 1963; their son, the fifth Ben Bennett, would be born in 1964 and a daughter Jane followed in 1966. The fifth Ben Bennett would join his father in the company in 1982, followed by his sister Jane in 1988. Today, with five children in the next generation, the family business looks set to continue indefinitely.

But the Bennett family is not the only family to have contributed to the long term success of the company. In 1995 the Board of Directors was made up of Ben Bennett the fourth, his wife Norma, their children, Ben and Jane, and Philip Udell. Philip Uddel had joined the company in 1952 as a new Company Secretary and held that post until his son, another Philip took over the role in 1989. The elder Philip Udell had been made a Director in 1971 and remained on the Board until his death in 2002; his son would in turn became a director the following year.

Today with some 70 employees many aspects of the business have remain unaltered, though the company no longer pickles, rolls and anneals steel at the Rolling Mills. The youngest Ben Bennett, with his wife Linzie, and his sister Jane, with her husband David, are responsible for bringing in the raw materials finished rolled from Germany. For quality and service few if any other

suppliers can compete and Grange Mill continues to supply the glass, rubber and chemical industries whilst the company's transport department has become very profitable with a fleet of vehicles of up to 30 tonnes capacity carrying scrap metal, sand, gravel and, in season, even potatoes and sugar beet.

Danecourt, the company's head office in Lisle Road, was built in 1926 as the Bennett family home. Although the building has been used as offices since 1938 its very existence serves as a solid reminder to all who enter that Rotherham's Ben Bennett Jr Ltd was not simply founded as a family firm in the 19th century but that it emphatically intends to continue to be one far into the 21st century!

Top left: Three generations of Ben Bennett Jr Ltd.
Top right: A family outing for the grandchildren at Rotherham United's Millmoor Ground in March 2004.
Below left: Family Directors, Ben Bennett (seated) his son Ben, wife Norma and daughter Jane. Below: The full Board Of Directors, the Bennett family and Philip Udell (back row left).

Muck and brass ... and much more

Over the course of more than three decades the name Ron Hull has become an increasingly familiar one to Rotherham residents. Today there is not simply one business bearing the Ron Hull name but a Group of companies.

The oldest company in the Group is Ronald Hull Junior Ltd which is involved in waste recycling, iron and steel processing, ferrous and non-ferrous metals and skip hire. Birkhull Engineering Ltd is a structural and cladding contractor, a skip body builder and is involved in design and fabrication. Ron Hull (Demolition/Excavation) Ltd has a self explanatory role whilst RHJ Developments Ltd is involved in the acquisition of both land and businesses. Meadowhall Landfill Ltd offers clients tipping facilities whilst MPM Logistics Ltd is a processor of exotic metals as well as offering customers storage and haulage services.

The founder of Ronald Hull Junior Ltd, and the Ron Hull Group, is, unsurprisingly the eponymous Ron Hull. A very private man, Ron commenced business in the early part of 1973 in waste disposal with a small ferrous metals recycling yard. The waste business remains a major contributor to the profits of what has over the years become a Group of Companies. The ferrous metal business however has grown substantially with the company's principal customer Corus, to whom the company supplies with upwards of 6,000 tonnes of processed material each month throughout the year for its furnaces.

In some ways 1973 was not a propitious year to start a new business venture. Inflation was in double figures and rising, whilst industrial unrest was reaching crippling levels with strikes in the power generation industry leading to Edward Heath's infamous three day week. Unemployment too was on the rise. OPEC had recently increased the price of crude oil to a point which was crippling western economies. 'We're all doomed' might well have been the catch phrase of the year. And just a few years previously the gloomiest of the gloomy were the members of the so-called Club of Rome.

Top left: *Founder Ron Hull.*
Left: *Ron Hull standing alongside a company shear.*
Below: *A familiar sight to the people of Rotherham, one of Ron Hull's fleet.*

entrepreneurs with the drive and flair to make such plants efficient.

In its fledgling days Ron Hull's business operated from a one acre site at Mangham Road, Parkgate in Rotherham, where just six people were employed.

The Group of companies still operates from Mangham Road but now from two parallel sites which in total cover some 30 acres of factory premises, prestigious offices and a state of the art waste transfer station.

Over the years the once small undertaking has expanded into the group of companies whose activities include engineering, non ferrous metal recovery, recycling of clean waste wood, ground reclamation, property development, leisure, plant hire, demolition, dismantling, asbestos removal and excavation.

The Club of Rome was a think tank made up of prominent economists who predicted the virtual decline of western civilisation. Their basic premise was that raw materials for industry were being consumed at such a rate that within a generation or two the Earth's resources would be exhausted: in particular oil, upon which world industry depended for power, would last for little more than a single generation.

With a combined annual turnover in excess of £19 million the Group provides employment for almost 200 people, mostly from the Rotherham area, and generates millions of pounds for the local economy.

The Group Chairman is ably assisted in the management of the business by his three sons, David, Nigel and Mark who are now Directors.

Happily for us oil supplies have lasted rather longer than predicted by the pessimistic members of the Club of Rome. But though the economists may have been wrong about supplies of crude oil the message was driven home that the Earth's resources are finite and needed to be husbanded carefully. That concept would collectively become known as the 'Green movement' and was reflected in an increasing interest in recycling everything from waste paper to glass bottles.

This page: *Ron Hull's new Leimbach 1000 Ton Static Shear.*

Recycling scrap metal was of course nothing new. Anyone who needs a reminder of that has only to look at the many walls still remaining in Rotherham which once featured iron railings but which were donated for recycling into munitions during the course of second world war.

What was new in the early 1970s was a sudden appreciation that as raw materials became ever harder to extract from the ground then the value of those which could be recovered and recycled would inevitably increase, making investment in recycling particularly attractive to

Ron Hull, supported by his wife Vivien, is proud of his Rotherham roots and has repeatedly demonstrated his abiding commitment to the town.

Several years ago Ron bought part of what used to be the 'stocking ground' of the long gone former Rotherham Power station. Later a smaller parcel of adjoining land was acquired from the Fitzwilliam (Wentworth) Estates increasing the area of land to some 16 acres.

Starting in 1996 with a successful planning application the former eyesore would be turned into a prime site for redevelopment following an extensive clean up operation which included ash, minerals and clay removal, coal extraction, inert in-fill and final compaction and certification.

In 1991 Ron Hull bought a derelict site on Mangham Road which had previously housed a chemical plant. This presented a major challenge but one which was grasped with his legendary enthusiasm. In just over two years a prestigious development of 13 business units together with a suit of offices for Ron Hull (Demolition/Excavation) Ltd was commissioned, and by 1994 were ready for occupation.

A little later Ron would go on to purchase the well known, but by then derelict, scissors factory on Infirmary Street. Applying his usual visionary approach to the factory Ron demolished the old building and ten flats were built for rent by local people.

The company founder's venture into the leisure industry began with the acquisition of the Fitzwilliam Arms Hotel on Mangham Road; this would become yet another example of Ron's determination to make things better for the local environment.

Top: *Loading wood into the Wood Chipper.*
Above: *The moulding of Aluminium ingots.*

In 1994 the Fitzwilliam Arms was, like many other local public houses, in terminal decline. Once purchased by Ron Hull however the hotel was soon restored to its former glory. The development now boasts a function room, children's playground, affordable food and provides an entertainment venue for the local area. The final piece in the redevelopment jig-saw followed a few years later with the completion of 18 tastefully decorated and competitively priced fully en-suite bedrooms.

A former director of Rotherham United Football Club Ron Hull sponsors Rotherham Rugby Club and donates generously to other amateur sports groups and local good causes.

Meanwhile the Ron Hull Group offers a 'One stop service' to the business community, Local Authorities, iron, steel and coal industries.

The Group's mananagment is passionate about preserving the environment - and the services they provide are carried out to the exacting standards Ron himself has set for them.

Inevitably the Group invests heavily in new plant, equipment, transport and techniques to ensure it maintains its competitive edge and continues to set and meet standards others seek to match.

One result of Chairman Ron Hull's focused approach is that recycling, a previously labour intensive business,has been transformed into a capital intensive operation resulting in a markedly more efficient service to customers.

The Group has membership of the British Metals Recycling Association, the National Federation of Demolition Contractors, the Wood Recycling Association and the British Safety Council: it has won national safety awards on no fewer than six occasions.

In 1998, in recognition of his achievements, Chairman Ron Hull was presented with an award for commitment to Rotherham Success at a function organised by the Rotherham Chamber of Commerce, Training and Enterprise.

Since then the Group has received other prestigious awards such as Contractor of the Year Award given by the Castle Vale Housing Action Trust, Birmingham and the Considerate Constructors Bronze Award for the site at Castle Vale.

The Group is a Licensed waste carrier, and is probably the North of England's largest waste manager, whilst the Group's demolition division Ron Hull (Demolition/Excavation) Ltd is amongst the top ten demolition contractors in the United Kingdom.

The Group's long term sustainabilty and growth has been partly due to well researched markets and an active approach to new business opportunities. Today with its non-adversarial attitude combined with a drive to push ahead with its Environmental Programme the Group is confident that it can continue to grow as the 21st century unfolds.

Top: *Ron Hull's Mangham Works site.*
Left: *A family portrait, Ron and Vivien Hull and their sons David, Nigel and Mark.*

A brush with history

There was a time when shops seemed to delight in hanging interesting items outside their premises. Shoemakers might use a huge boot as a business sign, opticians an oversize pair of glasses, or a jewellers' a large ornate clock. How many readers can still recall the big brush which once hung above the doorway of Russums brushmakers in Bridgegate? It was one of the most memorable bits of 'street furniture' in Rotherham. Generations of small children imagined that it must have been left hanging there by a passing giant!

E Russum & Sons Ltd can trace its origins in Rotherham back to 1830 when Thomas Mason established himself as a brush maker. By the early 1870s Mason's business had been bought by Charles Ward, listed as a brush maker and toy dealer in local directories. Trading from 20 Bridgegate the firm was known as 'Ward, Late Mason' for around the next ten years until Charles Ward became confident enough in his reputation to begin trading entirely under his own name.
Meanwhile in the late 1860s Edward Russum, the son of William Russum, a partner in Russum Bros. a brush manufacturer in Leeds, had completed his apprenticeship. Subsequently venturing south to Rotherham, by 1880 Edward Russum had acquired the 'Ward, late Mason' business, changing the name to E Russum and trading as a wholesale brush manufacturer. In the 1890s Edward moved across the street to 29 Bridgegate where the business would remain for almost 100 years until moving to new premises in 1982.

About the turn of the century Edward was joined by his son, another Edward, popularly known as Ned. The business was incorporated as E Russum & Sons Ltd in 1906. Ned had three sons, Ralph, George and Philip. Though George was killed on a ship torpedoed in the Irish Sea during the First World War, Ralph and Philip both followed

Above right: Transport in the early 20'h century. Ned Russum, accompanied by his young brother Roger, pose for the camera in the early years of the last century.
Right: Where it all began - Ward late Mason, brush manufacturers, can just be seen on the extreme right of this 19th century photograph.

their father into the family business during the twenties and thirties, remaining involved for the next 50 years.

After the first world war the firm gradually acquired adjoining properties, eventually owning 25-29 Bridgegate, giving the shop the impressive frontage which would be a familiar aspect of the street for many decades. In addition to the retail premises various workshops and old houses that bordered New Zealand Yard were also bought, providing manufacturing and warehouse capacity for the wholesale side of the business. By chance one of those houses enjoyed a small claim to fame, having been the birthplace on 30th January 1900 of Sandy Powell, the local comedian famous for his radio catch phrase 'Can you hear me, Mother?' Having made his stage debut at the age of seven Sandy was awarded the MBE in 1975 and was still working in the theatre when he died at the age of 82.

In 1948, Russums formed a subsidiary company, Hodgson & Powell Ltd., the title being derived from the name of a long standing employee in the brush works and the comedian who had been born on the premises. Likely one of Sandy Powell's less well known claims to fame.

Meanwhile the company's reputation for fine quality brushes had spread widely. A glance at a list of Russums' customers in the 1930s reads like a Who's Who of Rotherham's industrial past: Gummers Ltd at Effingham Valve works on Rawmarsh Road; Steel, Peach & Tozer Ltd. at Templeborough and the Parkgate Iron & Steel Co. Ltd. being just three well known if sadly now long defunct customers for Russum's 'Spade Brand' brushes. Further afield customers included the Cravens Railway Carriage & Wagon Co Ltd in Sheffield, Charles Roberts & Co Ltd at Wakefield and Brush Coachwork Ltd in Loughborough, all well known coach builders requiring specialist paint and varnish brushes to finish their vehicles to the highest standards. During the 1930s both Cravens and Roberts supplied bus bodies to the corporation transport, Russums having supplied the brushes to paint these vehicles. When subsequently repainted in the transport works at Rawmarsh Road 'Spade Brand' brushes were again used, with entries such as 'Russum, E & Sons brushes £1 6s 9d' (£1.34) being regular items amongst 'accounts to be paid' in the minutes of the Transport Committee.

On the retail front, from the earliest days, the industrial brushes had been supplemented by the sale of domestic brushes, quality hardware and household goods. Accordingly, from the shop in Bridgegate, the housewife could choose from a fascinating range of sweeping, hand and scrubbing brushes to assist her daily chores about the home. Alternatively, distemper, whitewash and paperhangers' brushes were

available for the more occasional tasks. All these brushes would have been manufactured with traditional wooden handles, the fillings obtained from natural fibres, fixed with wire, or alternatively set in glue or rubber.

Complementing the brushes was a whole range of quality hardware. Russum's list of the 'thirties, includes many now unfamiliar terms, a reminder of how life has changed in the last seventy years. Enamelware included five sizes of chamber pots and a slop pail, all essential before the advent of indoor toilets. To stock the legendary 'brick privy' there was a choice of Bronco, Jeyes and Izal toilet paper, together with such products as Sanizal to disinfect the facilities and even Cardinal to whiten the step, likely important when crossing the backyard in the dark. Galvanised products included household buckets, coal pans and baths. The latter were supplied eight different sizes of oval bath, together with two lengths of long oblong baths, all from an era before houses had bathroom facilities. These baths would have usually been used in front of the traditional fire, for which a variety of shovels was available, including three sizes of long handled coal shovel and four types of fire shovel. Along with the galvanised coal pans, all items unlikely to feature in the modern home, other than for purely decorative purposes. An even more obscure entry was a pothole shovel, sufficiently popular to be stocked in two qualities, being used to fuel the fire underneath the set-pot on wash days. Obviously Russums supplied a whole range of hardware associated with wash days, a fine little advert that survives in the archives implores our forebearers:

'REAL VALUE. Every housewife should get this splendid washing set. It's a real wonder bargain. The outfit consists of 1 best quality, full sized, hooped galvanised tub; 1 washboard with zinc panel; 2 dozen clothes pegs; 1 solid copper vacuum washer head; 1 clothes line 27 yards and 1 union laundry brush'

Top: *Russum's old shop in Bridgegate for nearly 100 years the registered office and an 'Aladdin's Cave' of brushes, quality hardware and household goods. The trademark brush, that hung above the door all those years, still survives (inset) inside the premises today.*

definitely long before automatic washing machines. The list of wooden ware is a reminder of other wash day essentials, such as sliding and long props, a staggering choice of five sizes of two, three or four fold clothes horses and the option of five leg or six leg peggies. Unknown today, the peggy was used to swish the clothes about in the tub, a real reminder of the hard work once associated with wash days.

Elsewhere around the kitchen, a wide range of household goods was available from Russum's old shop. Swan brand aluminium, in addition to saucepans, fry pans and colanders, listed a range of kettles, including whistling kettles, all now replaced by electric versions. Enamelware featured very prominently with a vast range of goods. Again, in addition to the still familiar saucepans, fry pans and colanders, such diverse items brawn moulds, ewers (a large water jug with a wide spout) and tea cans were all stocked. Traditionally, all enamelware would have been white though, by the late 'thirties, indicative of colours that would eventually be standard in the kitchen, Judgeware were offering a limited selection of the more popular products in ivory and green. Though only a small selection of the goods available, the above might hopefully provide a small reminder of the vast array of products in the Bridgegate shop. Obviously updating its range over the years, the business survived the Second World War, continuing in the 'fifties and 'sixties with Ralph Russum looking after the wholesale business, whilst Philip Russum took charge of the shop. Throughout these years, some additional management was provided by Rowland Sowden, who joined the business in the 'thirties and enjoyed a very long career, finally retiring in the 'seventies. With a style that would likely be difficult to repeat in the modern world, this versatile individual ran the office side of the business, whilst equally actively involved with the brush making and manufacturing.

In 1960 Philip's son, Peter, the present managing director, joined his father and uncle, eventually guiding the business through some momentous changes, during the next forty years. With steel and associated industries in decline, the market for industrial brushes was already getting less. Accordingly, fresh pastures were urgently needed, if the business was to grow and prosper. Two new avenues, both developments from existing activities, were further explored. Cocoa fibre door mats and matting had been sold from the earliest times, a natural progression in the late 'sixties, being to adopt a modern version, with the cocoa fibre set in a plastic backing, that could be bought on rolls and the individual mats cut to size as required. Under the guidance of Peter Russum, an early illustrated leaflet and price list was produced, being dispatched to likely customers throughout the country, the response giving Russums, for the first time in it's life, a national repertoire of customers, equally the confidence to explore further.

Another of Russum's traditional manufacturing activities, quietly undertaken in the maze of old buildings at the rear of the Bridgegate premises, had been the making of market stall covers and lorry sheets. To service this production, there was a stock of materials such as cotton duck, jute tarpaulin and hessian, together with the machines to sew these heavy cloths. Accordingly, when Rotherham College, which bought knives for catering students, required a means to store these 'weapons' in sets, suitable materials and sewing expertise were

Top: *Old receipts from Charles Ward, who was already dealing in items other than brushes by 1880 and E. Russum who was advertising himself as a woodware, twine and hardware merchant in 1901.* ***Far left:*** *An early letterhead- proudly boasting being 'Makers of Spade Brand Brushes and wholesale hardware merchants'.*
Left: *Russum brushes - a page from an early catalogue, showing spoke brushes and motor wing brushes; hair and clothes brushes, together with an early Addis toothbrush, part of the diverse range stocked in the 'thirties.*

the fifth generation of the family to be involved. Building on the sound foundations established by their father, the business continues to grow and prosper, the changes being well exemplified by the catalogue, the modest duplicated price list of the 'seventies having evolved into a fully illustrated colour brochure. 'Russums Catalogue 2004' would feature features one hundred pages of chef's clothing, professional knives, catering equipment and books. If the 'thirties customer list read like a 'Who's Who' of the town's industrial past, today's equivalent might be a 'Who's Who' of the country's catering colleges, hotels and restaurants.

available, to produce a slotted canvas knife wallet. Thus, during Peter's early career, he logically wondered where other colleges obtained knives, dutifully visiting both Doncaster College and Granville College in Sheffield, being rewarded with orders for sets of knives in canvas wallets. As always, following the Russum tradition of providing a good quality product, at a fair price and supported by attentive service, word spread and other colleges were steadily included on the list of annual customers. Moreover, in difficulties with unreliable supplies from London, the head of catering at Granville College, persuaded the 'local man' to kit out his students with their chef's jackets, trousers, aprons, etc. Thus, by the early 'seventies, with these early contacts and a fledgeling duplicated catalogue, the basis of today's extensive business was being established, very important to provide the confidence to face further changes in the coming years.

Meanwhile, local industry continued to decline, obviously adversely affecting traditional sales. Equally, during the late 'seventies, there was talk of redeveloping the north side of Bridgegate. In the event, the premises were compulsorily purchased, hastening the decision to abandon the retail trade and concentrate on the catering business. Therefore, after nearly one hundred years, connections with Bridgegate were severed, new purpose built premises at Tenter Street, being occupied in 1982.

Happily, the business has continued to prosper. Continuing a tradition that can be traced to the 'thirties and earlier, the canvas knife wallets are still a very important part of production together with a miscellany of hats, aprons and other small items of chef's uniform. By contrast, very different from the traditional activities, albeit still sewing related, are the four and six head computer operated embroidery machines, that daily personalise chef's jackets for customers throughout England, Scotland, Wales and beyond.

Likewise, perpetuating tradition, Peter's daughter Sally joined the business in 1993, followed by son Richard four years later,

Top left: *The first knife wallet produced at Tenter Street - as related elsewhere, the canvas knife wallets represent a fascinating link between the past and present. In this picture, the late Connie Sanders is sewing the first wallet in the new work room, June 19th, 1982, the finished product complete with knives can be seen inset. Like many others; past and present, Mrs Sanders had been a loyal employee of many years. Instrumental in converting the sewing room to clean products for the catering industry, by this stage she had only a couple more years service, before a well earned retirement.*
Below: *Russums catalogue 2004 - in complete contrast to earlier years, the catalogue is entirely devoted to chef's*

clothing, professional knives; catering equipment and books representing the vast changes in the business during the last forty years; as related in the text!.
Bottom: *Transport in the early 2lst century - like the products, the transport arrangements have seen enormous changes over the years, the Ford Transit Connect van being in sharp contrast to Ned Russum's horse drawn conveyance.*

Seven million miles and rising

So who in Rotherham drives more than seven million miles each year? Edward Pawson and his son Ernest that's who. We're cheating of course. It's really the drivers of the Rotherham haulage firm E Pawson & Son Ltd who really do that stupendous annual mileage in a whole fleet of lorries; both E Pawson and his son have long since passed away, though happily the firm remains safely in the hands of their descendants.

Pawson's distinctive red liveried vehicles based at Fieldhouses, Braithwell, have long been a familiar sight around Rotherham and the surrounding area. Indeed the family name goes back in the immediate locality to at least as far as 1397 when the West Riding Poll Tax records show Nicholaus Paweson, a 'bakester' and his wife, the delightfully-name Idonia, being assessed for tax of one shilling (5p), some three times higher than the standard rate of tax. It seems the Pawsons have always had an entrepreneurial streak.

Edward Ernest Pawson (1878-1958), the great grandfather of the present managers, and his son Charles Ernest Pawson (1903-1970), always

called Ernest by locals, moved to the site of the present business at Fieldhouses, Braithwell in 1921, renting a cottage there and 21 acres of land. The haulage side of the business began shortly afterwards, with the pair carrying coal from Maltby Colliery and delivering around the local area by horse and cart.

Before starting the haulage business Edward Pawson had earlier worked as a gardener for Lord Scarborough, whilst his son Ernest had worked in the lamp cabin at the Maltby Colliery.

Had the father and son known what lay in store from them just around the corner however they might well have had second thoughts about setting up in business for themselves. On the face of it 1921 seemed an excellent year to begin a new enterprise, yet in retrospect we can see that the 1920s and 1930s were far from being the best of times for anyone to try and start a new business. The brief economic boom which had followed the cessation of hostilities in 1918 was followed all too soon by a recession which would eventually see 3 million unemployed. The General Strike of 1926 saw demand for transport come to a virtual halt for some time, whilst the Wall Street Crash of 1929 heralded the collapse of much of the world economy. Men who had fought in the 'war to end wars' between 1914 and 1918 found work hard to come by

Top left: Mr & Mrs Edward Ernest Pawson.
Centre: One of the first lorries acquired by Pawsons. Below: Fieldouses, Braithwell in 1970. Right: Pea loading, 1959.

and unhappily discovered all too soon that the government had little idea how to tackle the nation's terrible economic ills. Fortunately for the Pawsons there was still some work about, even if it was hard to come by.

At first the new transport business was run with a horse and cart, but a one ton Ford lorry was eventually acquired which was used, amongst other things, for carrying building supplies for new miners homes being built in Maltby.

The company was an early member of the Associated Road Operators organisation which later became the Road Haulage Association - being one of the founding members with membership number No. 16.

The business steadily increased over the years helped, not least, by Ernest's wife Mary (1911-1996) who helped answering telephones as the business was run from home.

Though in the war years between 1939 and 1945 many small haulage companies suffered through lack of fuel; Pawson's were able to continue in business since their activities by now included moving livestock for which they were granted special allocation of fuel. Indeed the firm was one of the first local haulage businesses to start moving livestock.

In 1970 Charles Ernest Pawson died; though having been born in Carlton-in-Lindrick before moving to Sandbeck Park when his father began working for Lord Scarborough he had lived in Braithwell for fifty years; he had played an integral part in the life of the village having been member of the Parish Council for 18 years, serving as chairman on three separate occasions. He was one of the founders of the Braithwell 'Good Companions' an organisation formed to support local charities and he was an enthusiastic worker for all welfare work in the village. Ernest was also a Freemason, as well as having been a keen sportsman and he still retained a love for sport until his death

Following Ernest's death the company passed to the present directors, his sons Arnold and Derrick who now took over complete control of the business. Until the 1960s Derrick had been a driver whilst his brother Arnold had helped Ernest in the office. Between them they would continue to expand the business which by now was some forty years old.

The firm became a limited company in 1974 and today employs over 100 staff and operates an extensive fleet

Top left: Transporting pigeons for the Doncaster & District Federation of Homing Pigeon Societies.
Top right: Transporting hay, circa 1960.
Left: Ernest Pawson (front middle) with sons Derrick and Arnold behind him.

of vehicles offering deliveries from just a single pallet up to 26, and from one tonne to 30 tonnes.

It is now run on a daily basis by the family's fourth generation, Arnold's sons Michael and Richard, together with Derrick's children Stephen and Rachel, though Derrick and Arnold remain active as directors of the company.

Before joining the family firm Stephen had trained with Crossroads Commercials, the Volvo dealers as an HGV fitter, Rachel had originally gone into retail management whilst Richard had been an auto electrician and Michael came straight from school.

Though still at the same address after more than 80 years extensive building works have altered the site beyond recognition: a new workshop, block paving and a quality perimeter fence for increased site security.

Today E Pawson & Son Ltd specialises in deliveries to supermarkets with contracts to carry goods for many of the largest names in the food industry.

The firm prides itself in providing a service second to none and with health and safety a priority. Having invested heavily in equipment used in the food industry the present generation of managers believe they now have the edge

Top right: *Long heavy and high loads can all be accommodated by Pawson's specialised fleet.* **Above right:** *E Pawson & Son Ltd take delivery of two new Mercedes, 2002.* **Below:** *One of Pawsons Curtainsiders for quick and easy loading.*

over their commercial rivals and will continue to expand not only in the food sector but also in warehousing.

Now as a member of Pall-ex the country's leading pallet network, delivering smaller loads of palletised freight across the UK. Pawson Pall-ex offers customers a next day

delivery between one and six pallets or even larger consign-ments throughout all parts of the country. Some 90 hauliers arrive each night at the Pall-ex 'Hub' where pallets are sorted for swapping and re loaded on the appropriate vehicle which can then deliver them the next day.

Things have certainly moved on since Pawson's early horse and cart days. Dry insulated secure, and sealable box vans are used by customers for high value goods; a 'curtainsider' fleet offers customers quick and easy loading for dry freight with internal side apertures nearly three metres wide and the opportunity of double stacking for lighter loads. The company has a particular speciality in agricultural haulage. Pawson's offers a facility for sugar beet cleaning and loading, or delivery only. As a large haulier group the company has tremendous flexibility; and by being a representative on the committee at both York and Newark sugar beet factories to which the group delivers the company enjoys excellent working relationships with British Sugar staff from fieldsmen to factory managers.

Meanwhile away from agricultural and into the industrial sector E Pawson & Son also has an extensive fleet of trailer s to meet every need. Long , heavy and high loads can all be accommodated with a specialised fleet of low loaders, extending and multi axle trailers plus 'cat 2' plated tractor units operated by highly experienced and competent drivers. Flat trailers of all types are available too to match all customers' differing needs. Drivers are trained to rope and sheet to secure and keep loads dry in all weather conditions.

Drivers are also trained to use chains and straps for the more awkward and unusual loads.

What the company's founders would make of all this is hard to imagine. In 1921 they began the business with only a horse and cart and for the next two decades struggled to survive years of economic depression. A fleet of half a dozen motor vehicles would have seemed like a miracle to them - they would surely never have imagined that one day lorries bearing their names would be travelling more than seven million miles each year.

Top: Now a member of Pall-Ex, E Pawsons & Son deliver smaller loads of palletised freight throughout the UK.
Below: E Pawson & Son Ltd's home, Fieldhouses, Braithwell, Rotherham. Bottom: Part of the Pawson fleet.

Nuts about Rotherham

What would a world be like without KP salted peanuts? Those delicious bags of peanuts have been with us since 1953. But why are they called 'KP' nuts? That's one of those fascinating philosophical mysteries that must have occupied the minds of millions as they contentedly enjoyed one of life's greatest treats.

Although KP has been producing its famous nuts at its home on Chesterton Road, Eastwood for over half a century, the firm which began it all, Kenyon, Son and Craven, had been in Rotherham since 1853 founded by Charles Kenyon.

The business was sold in the late 1940s to Simon Heller. Originally from Lithuania, Mr Heller came from the East End of London where his father, a rabbi, sold sweets and nuts from a handbarrow.

At the start of the 1950s the ailing company sold pickled onions, jams, gobstoppers and other types of sweets. Simon Heller had an arrangement with a friend in the Sheffield Market who would tip him off when there was a glut, enabling him to take a van to the market in the afternoon to stock up on cheap vegetables. Then there would be a rush at the factory to cut and pickle and to make chutney.

At that time sugar was still difficult to get, and what little could be obtained was used for making nougat and pan work to make it go as far as possible. The factory eked out its supply by making liquorice comfits and chlorodyne gums.

Above: KP's eight different varieties of nuts.
Below: An old style Nut Sorter machine.

After years of war-induced hardship Simon Heller's imagination and unrelenting economies were beginning to pay off for the firm. In 1952 the share capital which had been just £50,000 in £1 shares was doubled to £100,000.

As more sugar supplies became available the pickling side of the business was phased out. Obtaining sugar was still far from easy however. Sugar syrup was being imported to the UK via Holland but Simon Heller decided to cut out the middle man and set up a factory in Barbados to make sugar syrup there. It was however a risk: hundreds of drums filled with syrup stood immobile of the quays until an import licence was obtained. According to company legend a production shortcut involved turning the sugar into syrup by the simple expedient of adding water and having the barrels rolled all the way to the quayside. Once in the UK the sugar syrup was sold to grateful confectionery manufacturers all over the country.

Products were sold under different trade names - sweets under the name of Duncan & Dawson, and peanuts originally as Hercules Nuts.

The market for nuts was growing. In 1953 the now legendary twopenny packet of KP Nuts was introduced as the first nationally distributed nut line.

Other products at the factory such as Lucky Bags would gradually be pushed out as nut processing increased.

New machinery was virtually unobtainable, and the country was scoured for second hand equipment. A small gas frying machine was bought and used to cook the firm's restricted supply of nuts. In 1948 hazelnuts were the first post war nuts to become available on the free market, and the chance had been seized: roasted and salted they were delivered direct to shops and to cinemas. If a customer was short then fresh supplies were sent at any time, including late in the evening.

In 1950 the original factory in Morpeth Street, by then a very old building, had been acquired for an extension to the College of Technology . The business moved to its new home on the Eastwood trading estate with Simon Heller filling the boot of his own car with invoices and papers to help the move.

Top left: *KP and McVities product being viewed by the Mayor of Rotherham in 1979.*
Top right: *Miss KP 1978-79.*
Right: *Employees sorting through the raw nuts, removing stalks etc.*

By 1962 continuous frying was introduced. Two batch fryers had a maximum output of eight hundredweight an hour. Continuous frying now raised that output, first to 15 hundredweight, then 25 and later to two tons an hour.

Technical credit for building KP's own plant for processing nuts went to Maurice Cohen a former chief development engineer with Rowntrees who had joined KP nuts in 1956. Maurice Cohen, an engineer of unique ability, pioneered the application of a high standard of technology to production to achieve a standard product instead of a variable one. At the start of the 1960s KP Nuts was a poor market second, by the end of the decade the company would be the market leader.

Simon Heller's son Michael joined the company in 1961, at the start of what he would later describe as a golden age, a period which would see a small struggling business become a household name.

Packets of peanuts may seem ordinary items but they have surprisingly exotic associations. South America, the Caribbean, India and Hong Kong were amongst the many places scoured by KP employees in search of the best nuts in the world. The first post war imports of peanuts had been from Uganda, the second from Tanganyika, setting of the British Government's ill-starred Ground Nuts Scheme - though not so ill-starred that it stopped KP buying up the whole crop one year. By the 1970s however KP would source most of its nuts from Malawi - a source which continues to dominate to this day in addition to Australia and Paraguay.

KP's developing strength took a huge leap forward in 1962 when Marks & Spencer asked the company to produce its St Michael brand of nuts and fruit and nuts: the association sparked off a dramatic leap forward in production - and in production techniques when M&S demanded that it be supplied only with whole peanuts. A similar technological leap forward

would be required when the Council demanded that peanut skins be no longer flushed away into the sewerage system which was becoming blocked by the volume produced: a new dry-skinning method produced a surprising extra profit from selling the skins as cattle food.

Marks and Spencer were the first retailers to introduce 'Best by' date-coding to food products, and KP

*Top: A photograph showing employees in the old style uniforms. **Above:** Miss KP Rotherham receives a bouquet of flowers from the Mayoress of Rotherham.*

use the name for other products marketed by its food division in the snack market.

Over the years many new products would be introduced, some like dry roasted peanuts, a KP original, going on to great success; others like peanut butter and peanut brittle enjoyed less public interest. Novelty however continues to keeps the KP name at the forefront of public perception, and honey roasted nuts, Indian spices and sun dried tomatoes versions have all been introduced, alongside cashew nuts, walnuts and even chocolate peanuts.

However innovative the company may be though, surely nothing will ever match the unrepeatable perfection of the original KP salted peanuts which are still produced at the rate of more than 17,000 tons a year by today's workforce of 327 staff at the highly automated Chesterton Road factory - though such is the pace of technological change that a mere 45 now actually work on nut production.

And lastly, why are they called 'KP' nuts? That's simple, it's just a short-hand reminder of the original firm 'Kenyon Products'.

consequently also become one of the first British firms to introduce such an innovation. As part of its continuous attention to product quality KP even introduced a system whereby its salesmen would take back unsold stock from retailers after ten weeks and replace it with new, at no cost to the retailer.

Unsurprisingly between 1964 and 1966 KP doubled the size of its factory. By the time the company was sold to United Biscuits in 1968 for £3.5 million it was enjoying a turnover of some £5 million annually. Michael Heller, then aged 32, joined the board of United Biscuits (Holdings) Ltd and remained Managing Director of KP Nuts until 1970. Simon Heller, the man who made KP Nuts world famous, would die in 1989 at the age of 82.

By 1970 the factory was processing 500 tons of nuts each week, brought to the factory by barge from Hull. In 1943 the then tiny company employed around 50 people, by 1971 when it became a part of the United Biscuits foods Division some 1,500 staff were employed by KP in Rotherham.

Being acquired by United Biscuits benefited the factory through access to greater capital, marketing and technical resources. Production on a 24 hour basis raised output to seven tons of nuts an hour, a volume which supplied 70 per cent of the market.

So successful would be the KP brand that United Biscuits later took the decision to

*Top: A final check before despatch **Below:** The home of KP Nuts, Chesterton Road, Eastwood Industrial Estate, Rotherham.*

Plastering Paris

What's the connection between Rotherham and Mickey Mouse? And no smart answers please. The unexpected answer is that faux Victorian columns from Rotherham can be found at the EuroDisney complex in France.

The columns were completed by Lloyd Clough & Sons based in Sumner Road Rotherham. But its not just in EuroDisney that Rotherham magic can be found. Throughout Britain theme park operators and leisure centre mangers have been installing an extraordinary range of sculptures, columns, boulders and other exotic and imaginative architectural features designed in Rotherham and made from cement & sand Render and plaster.

Established in 1961 Lloyd Clough & Sons was originally a partnership between boyhood pals Lloyd Clough and Andrew Stevens - the company's original name being Clough & Stevens. In 1968 however Andrew Stevens left the business and the present name was adopted.

Lloyd's sons joined the company in the 1970s.

Raymond Clough joined the building industry as an apprentice in 1971. After a period of five years qualifying he continued to work on site for a further six years gaining the extensive practical skills that would be required for successful site management.

Terence Clough joined the company in 1974 after obtaining a Bachelor of Science degree from East Anglia University.

With Lloyd's experience, Raymond's practical knowledge and Terence's academic and technological expertise the family partnership was in a perfect position to provide a highly professional, quality service to the construction industry alongside Lee Cousins, a former silver trowel winning apprentice who joined the company in 1983 and is now also a director.

Company founder Lloyd Clough was born in 1930 in Herringthorpe where he grew up. At the age of 14 he became a butcher's boy but switched to become a plasterer's apprentice when he discovered that as a butcher's boy he couldn't take Saturdays off to play football.

*Top: Lloyd Clough & Sons Ltd's office, Sumner Road, Rotherham. **Below left:** Ray Clough 'The Gaffer' takes a well earned break and becomes the 'Tea Boy' in EuroDisney. **Below:** The Rotherham premises at Sumner Road were completely re-built in 1989.*

In the late 1980s a downturn in the construction industry was set to lead to redundancies, yet a contract with EuroDisney would save the day. Short of work in the United Kingdom the firm began to tender for jobs in Germany, Spain and France. EuroDisney needed someone to carry out high quality moulding work in cement render to the 84 'stone' columns in its main ticket hall. The Rotherham team certainly impressed the folk at Disney.

In 1948 Lloyd joined the Army for two years before returning to continue his plastering apprenticeship with local plasterer Thomas Fennerty. In the early 1950s Lloyd was ready to go full-time with the Rotherham Plastering Company with Pat and Jim Fennerty with whom he worked for three or four years until taking a job with Parkin & Co builders with whom he remained until starting out on his own with Andy Stevens in 1961.

During the 1960s the firm concentrated on construction work, plastering new houses as well as commercial projects such as police stations, hospitals and shops.

As expertise increased over the years projects became more involved: in the early 1970s for example the company was involved in refurbishing Bradford's St George's Hall. A later project involved providing all the mouldings for a new extension to the National Union of Miner's premises. Their skill and experience has been used to good effect on many of Rotherhams public buildings including The Police Headquarters on Main Street, Rotherham Magistrates Court, Rotherham District General Hospital, as well as most of Rotherhams Schools and Public Transport infrastructures.

But all was not plain sailing. In the late 1970s bankruptcies of major contractors led to losses of many thousands of pounds.

A second EuroDisney contract soon followed, this time to carry out moulded cement render work on the plinths around Main Street USA and on the facade of the Town Hall.

During those projects for EuroDisney the firm discovered it could use rendering to produce items that looked just like real rock - a discovery which would open up a whole range of new opportunities.

Today Lloyd Clough & Sons can look back on more than four decades of innovation in the plastering trade, and although much of the business continues to be in its traditional plastering services role it is surely its remarkable work in the field of architectural art and sculpture which will ensure that the firm remains permanently fixed in the Rotherham public's mind - not least as a result of the company's unique offices whose extraordinary facade immediately reminds visitors of Fred Flintstone's hometown of Bedrock and comes complete with purple dinosaur. Now that's magic.

Top, both picture: The Belfrey Public House (left) and Doncaster DHSS offices plastered by Lloyd Clough & Sons.
Above centre: An example of Lloyd Clough & Sons subsidiary 'Plasterland's' Adventure Golf themes.
Below left: Sponsors Lloyd Clough donated a cheque for £1,000 to Maltby Miners FC. *Below:* (L-R) Lloyd Clough, Raymond Clough and Terence Clough.

Happy Schooldays

Rudston Preparatory School in Rotherham's Broom Road first opened its doors to pupils on 19th April 1948. The school's founder was Mrs GA Butcher, a teacher and elocutionist, who was helped in the venture by her parents Mr and Mrs FJ Trotman: Mr Trotman was also one of the first teachers at the school. Today the school has some 46 staff but at the outset was staffed by just seven.

The school takes its name from Rudston House the original name of the premises; its first owners had enjoyed holidaying at Rudston in North Yorkshire and decided to give that name to their home. Before becoming a school the house had also been the home of Sir Donald Bailey, whose famous temporary bridges would be so useful during the course of the second world war.

At the time it began the school's aim was to give its pupils a thorough preparatory training to enable them to qualify for entry into public schools and local grammar schools.

Those who attended the school will recall being taken to the Schools Outfit Supply in Glossop Road, Sheffield, to be kitted out in the school's original grey and cherry uniform, later to be

changed to an even more distinctive grey and purple. No doubt former pupils also recall their parents taking them to get the rubber soled slippers or sandals which Mrs Butcher demanded for wear indoors. What children won't recall is their parents paying their £12 a term fees, plus an extra two guineas for private elocution lessons with the well spoken Mrs Butcher.

Good teachers soon helped pupil numbers rise. Since its founding the school has grown in both size and reputation to become one of the area's premier independent prep schools. The school would expand to take in next door, number 61 Broom Road, and later number 63 too. A pre-school branch has now opened at 81 Gerard Road.

Over the years former staff and pupils will have particularly fond memories of Anita Cartner who retired in July 1995 after running the school for a quarter of a century. No doubt today's generation of pupils will take away similar memories of Principal Sandra Atack who was head of the school until 2004.

Top: *Rudston Preparatory School's Coat-of-Arms and motto Optima Petite which translates Strive For The Best.*
Right: *Any early prospectus.*
Below: *A 1950 school photograph with founder Mrs GA Butcher centre picture.*

are below those of many other independent schools, whilst bursaries are available making private education more affordable. As for extra elocution lessons, they are part of the past.

The school caters for boys and girls from the age of two to eleven years, and offers a high standard of academic achievement together with a wide variety of extra-curricular activities and early morning and after school care facilities to support busy parents.

But whether they benefited from elocution lessons or not many former pupils have gone on to become successful doctors, lawyers and business men and women, whilst others, such as racing driver Justin Wilson, have achieved fame in other fields.

The school motto is Optima Petite - Strive For The Best: and when it comes to class sizes few would doubt the truth of that. With class sizes restricted to a maximum of 24 pupils Rudston school aims to live up to its motto.

The majority of pupils go on to major independent secondary schools and Rudston prepares children for entrance exams for these schools. The school is noted for its musical activities and all pupils have the opportunity to learn an instrument. The school choir takes part in festivals and performs throughout the area, whilst instrumentalists are encouraged to join the school orchestra. All pupils learn French from the age of four, culminating in a trip to France in their final year. Rudston has a growing reputation for the quality of its drama productions. Towards the end of each year the school's Drama Club and Choir are given the opportunity to perform in a professional theatre.

Top left: *Netball is just one of a wide range of activities taught at Rudston by specialist P.E. staff, others include; football, rugby, cricket, rounders, short tennis and athletics.* **Above left:** *Pupils learn Information Communication Technology.* **Top right:** *Children in Rudston's Pre-School department.* **Above (left):** *Pupils pose for a photograph at the school sign.* **Above (right):** *The Pre-Prep Department for 3+ pupils.* **Left:** *The music department where pupils have the opportunity to learn to play a wide range of instruments.*

Rudston is a small school that aims to provide an excellent education together with a warm family atmosphere, where all pupils can feel secure and happy, and can develop their full potential. And though fees may have risen somewhat since the days when Mrs Butcher made a charge of £12 a term, they

Lighting - brighter by design

Combining its skill and expertise in both design and manufacture, today Rotherham's ASD Lighting Plc provides a unique range of high quality lighting products.

Dr Rowan Williams the Archbishop of Canterbury may be the leading light of the Church of England, but when he needed an outside light for his Newport home he looked to South Yorkshire to illuminate his way with a lantern made in Rotherham.

In 1982 Applied Security Design Plc was a small electrical contracting company based over a shop in Sheffield. At the time more and more homes were being burgled. As a result, the company, then with just five employees, decided to offer an extra service; it would install burglar alarm equipment in properties as well as other electrics.

Top: Founder, Tony Stewart. Below: English Estates Regional Manager John Derbyshire congratulates Tony Stewart on becoming their 280th tenant. Right: National Sales Manager Ray Stewart exhibits ASD products. Bottom right: L-R Jon Finelli, Sales and Marketing Director of ASD, Colin Offer Executive Director of Sheffield Business Link and Tony Stewart MD of ASD receiving a Business Success Award for ASD Lighting Plc.

The business obtained an exclusive licence from a German company to install and distribute its then brand new Passive Infrared Detector (PIR). Demand for this product was greater than supply, and the company acquired the right to manufacture the product itself. According to founder and Managing Director, Tony Stewart 'There was reluctance from other businesses to manufacture the PIR, so, working alongside a postgraduate from Manchester University, we put together a prototype, which we then exhibited. The interest was tremendous and in 1984 we started to manufacture the sensor from a factory in Rotherham's Eastwood Trading Estate. Within six months we were employing 24 people.'

ASD originally only sold its products to the established burglar alarm market, but it now decided to move into the electrical wholesale market. The company fitted the sensor into a light fitting, and as a result, it was one of the first in the world to offer a PIR light fitting. Turnover soon rocketed towards one million pounds a year, and in 1986 the company moved to 10,000 square feet premises to house its now 50 staff.

At the same time, DIY companies such as Texas, Homebase, Do it All and B&Q had started trading, and ASD decided that they would be a good outlet. 'They were looking for new and innovative products,' says Tony. 'We supplied

By 2004 ASD would have over 170 employees. An experienced design team works alongside the company's research and development team in designing and developing innovative new products; its customer services department deal with any queries in fitting products. The business also has a team that gives free-of-charge technical back-up to help customers design lighting schemes and plan their installations, with no obligation to use ASD light fittings. Tony stresses 'Employing people with an exceptional knowledge and understanding of their area of responsibility is of great importance, whether it is in sales, accounts or production. We invest in professional people and training, and staff have the opportunity to move from the shop floor and into sales, meaning that they will already know about the products, and about the business as a whole. Although the company deals through the wholesaler, it ensures that the electrician always knows what ASD is doing and why, and assists them to take on board every new job, by providing comprehensive technical back-up'.

The ASD story is certainly no light achievement.

Texas with our own range of PIR lights products, such as the Guardlight and the Superflood, which is a flood light with a sensor. Over the next few years we achieved a three million pound turnover.'

By 1989 however, the DIY companies started to apply downward pressure on pricing, looking at cost rather than quality. ASD decided to turn its attention back to electrical wholesalers. The firm quit the retail market altogether and began to concentrate on creating a quality-engineered lighting business.

The gamble paid off; the factory was extended in 1990, whilst in 1999 another 32,000 sq ft was acquired on the Barbot Hall Estate. In 2003 the company bought a neighbouring factory providing another 42,000 sq ft as part of a £2 million investment plan.

Yet despite this massive expansion ASD remains a family firm: Tony's son Richard is Export Manager, Tony's brother Terry is Area Sales Manager, whilst nephew Ray is National Sales Manager.

Today, ASD designs, develops and sells all types of bespoke light fittings to the electrical wholesale market. The company would see a 25 per cent growth in its market over the first four years of the new millennium, pushing turnover towards £15 million .

Top left: *The ASD Sales Team.*
Top right: *Dr Rowan Williams the Archbishop of Canterbury leans on one of ASD's lights at his Newport home.* **Centre:** *Old and new ASD products.*
Below left: *CCTV machinery circuit boards being assembled by ASD staff.* **Below:** *The company premises, Mangham Road, Rotherham.*

The acid test

An acid test is guaranteed. One firm that has passed the acid test of time itself is Rotherham's Degussa Fine Organics chemical business, previously known as Laporte Fluorides.

It was about 1860 that James Wilkinson started his small chemical works in Tinsley Park Road Sheffield and in Attercliffe. His aim was to supply to steel works abounding in the area, many within easy carting distance, with the chemicals they needed - foremost amongst them the acids for pickling and dipping fabricated metal.

When James Wilkinson died the business was managed by his son Frank. In 1924 Frank Wilkinson sold out to Henry Ellison, who registered the company as James Wilkinson & Son Ltd.

The manufacturing range in 1925 included the obligatory nitric and hydrochloric acids in various strengths and purities, but the really specialised product was hydrofluoric acid which found particular application in the polishing, etching and frosting of glass and in the pickling of brass and stainless and other alloy steels. Wilkinson's employed about 40 people at the time. Wilkinson's supply of fluorspar first came from Derbyshire, and in particular, from 1935, from the Glebe mine in Eyam village.

Just before the war an enquiry came in which was to prove tremendously significant. It was from a company

in Birmingham and concerned potassium and sodium fluorborates as a technically convenient way of introducing boron into special metal alloys. The consequential business remained important to the firm for many years

As production expanded during and after the second world war more land was needed and a 12 acre site in Gin House Lane (the name deriving from a horse-driven winding engine or 'gin' once used in coal extraction) Rotherham was chosen, and a new works opened in 1948 in which the whole production of fluorides was concentrated.

In 1959 Laporte acquired the Sheffield Chemical Company Ltd as well as James Wilkinson and Son Ltd and Glebe Mines Ltd. It was hoped that they would provide Laporte an entry into fluorine chemicals.

Some facilities including offices and the preparation and bottling of pure acids remained at Tinsley Park Road, but by the mid-1960s all had been transferred to Rotherham.

By the time Laporte took over the Rotherham plant was making 4-5,000 tons a year of hydrofluoric acid, and within two years capacity was being enlarged further. Not only was hydrofluoric acid being sold to the established industries like steel alloy, but the popularity of the new transistor radio sets induced the company to make the purest hydrofluoric acid in Europe for the

*Top: The original site 1963. **Below left:** Construction work in progress, 1964. **Below:** The new office and laboratory block is completed, 1964.*

As markets became more competitive however, and technology advanced, changes and investment had to be made if the business was to continue. In 1994 money was made available to build a new effluent plant, and in the mid-1990s the product range was reduced significantly. The calciners which produced hydrofluoric acid were closed late in 1996 and a new reception facility was built to allow anhydrous hydrogen fluoride to be bought as the major raw material.

A year or so later the company quit the potassium fluoroborate and fluorotitanate markets and closed those plants to concentrate on more profitable products.

At the end of 1999 the DFDPM facility was sold to a major customer, Victrex Manufacturing Ltd, which continued to be an important partner.

The next few years saw considerable investment in the plants in terms of automation and upgrading, in staff through training and development and in customers through ever closer working relationships.

production of silicon and germanium, and for the etching of transistors and other semiconductor devices. From this point on Rotherham developed an important role as a supplier to the electronics industry.

In 1963 new potassium fluorides and fluoroborates units were commissioned, and a new office block became available in July. The new plant would ensure that the Rotherham site would become a significant profit maker for Laporte, and this was to continue throughout the 1980s.

A new organo fluoride, DFDPM, an 'intermediate' for a high performance polymer, which also used fluoroboric acid as a raw material, came on stream in 1985.

In 2001 Degussa acquired the whole of the Laporte business and what had been Laporte Fluorides now became Degussa Fine Organics, Rotherham.

Top left: *The Degussa plant by night.*
Top right: *A view inside the plant.*
Above left: *Charging a reactor.*
Below left and below: *The Degussa site entrance and reception*

JH Clark & Son

Is this the Oldest Surviving Family Owned Funeral Directors in the Country?
Established 1784

JH Clark & Son, Funeral Directors was established in Rawmarsh, Rotherham in 1784. Since that time it has been handed down by Father to Son spanning over five generations, it is still owned and managed by the Clark family, which is quite unique in this day and age. Graham Clark ably assisted by his two sons Richard and Matthew Clark provide the people of Rawmarsh and Rotherham with the Dignity and Respect this old established business has always been renowned for.

Top left: *A Taxi in the 1940s.*
Right: *A JH Clark invoice from 1933.*
Below: *JH Clark & Son, 46 High Street Rawmarsh, home of the company for over 300 years, 1960.*

The business is still operated and managed from the original stone built premises from which Joshua H Clark started over 300 years ago, it is one of the oldest surviving properties left on the High Street. Being a 24 hour service the family have lived and worked from the house which still retains many of the original features, in fact the old parish oven still exists behind one of the internal walls.

The business was founded in 1784 by Joshua H Clark a joiner, carpenter and wheelwright who hand-made coffins and transported them in his horse and cart. As a matter of course he agreed to 'undertake' all the arrangements for the bereaved families hence the term 'Undertaker' which over the years has been changed to Funeral Director. Times were different then with no motor transport or telephones the business was kept mainly local.

JH Clark & Son fully endorses this and tries to accommodate personal wishes where they are possible.

During the course of more than 300 years JH Clark & Son has been providing the people of Rawmarsh and Rotherham with kind of funeral they would wish for themselves and for their loved ones. Yorkshire folk have a long tradition of giving death the quiet respect it deserves and marking that final transition with due dignity. In the 21st century when many small firms of funeral directors have disappeared to be replaced by large, impersonal businesses it is reassuring to know that when a family suffers a bereavement they can still turn to another family for help. Generations have trusted the Clark family with making those final arrangements, and hopefully none have been disappointed by the professional and understanding manner with which the business has provided this, the ultimate service.

Modern technology has changed all that and now business is conducted all over the local area and the advent of the mobile phone now makes offering a 24 hour service much easier, ensuring that someone is always available to offer help when needed.

How times change over the years, the business started with a horse and cart and the relatives and friends would walk behind the cortege, a horse and carriage came next and with the advent of the motor car, a fleet of Rolls Royces, including a hearse and two limousines was acquired. The Clark women had always helped in the business but during and after the war Margaret Clark (Graham's mother) drove the cars which which were also being used as taxis as her husband Albert Clark was away overseas. The children also helped by mucking out and exercising the horses. The taxi service continued into the 1970s. The Rolls Royce fleet has over the years been replaced and today a Jaguar hearse and two SAAB limousines make up the fleet, but how times turn full circle as more and more people are requesting a horse and carriage again to take their loved ones on their final journey. Now in the 21st century people have more say and choice about what they want to happen to them on their final journey, and some people even plan and pay in advance as they themselves want to make their own arrangements to ensure they get exactly what they want. Being a family business

In 2000 the business expanded and acquired Johns Funeral Service in Thurcroft Near Rotherham though retaining the name. This also was a family business and John the former owner, although retired, still helps in the business occasionally.

As for the future: with two sons involved in the business, perhaps Rawmarsh, Rotherham, Thurcroft and surrounding areas will still be benefiting from the services of JH Clark & Son three hundred years from now.

Top left: *JH Clark & Son hearse and limousines, 1950s.*
Below: *Richard and Graham Clark pictured alongside the company hearse and limousines.*

From sunway to sun

Coach trips have come a long way over the last few decades. Older readers will recall coach trips to the seaside with endless choruses of 'Ten Green Bottles' being sung to pass the time. Drivers of what we used to call 'charas' had to be a hardy breed to put up with the same limited repertoire of songs repeated ad infinitum. But how times have changed.

Leger Holidays, based in Sunway House, Canklow Meadows was founded in 1982 by Alan Henry. Alan was a former school teacher and youth worker who had already been involved in the travel industry for some 15 years and now decided to go it alone.

Selling his holidays through newspapers adverts placed all across the country Alan's first holidays were 7-day coach tours to the Austrian Tyrol. In that first year 30,000 customers travelled with the firm, and often there would be up to 80 coaches on the road each week.

In the very early days the firm operated from Alan's home, and more particularly from his son Ian's bedroom. When Ian returned home from Leicester after his first term at university in October 1982 he

discovered his bedroom now housed a telex machine and had become a working office for his father and his mother Cynthia.

In subsequent years the range of destinations expanded to include the Italian Sud Tyrol, Germany's Rhine Valley and Harz Mountains, and Norway. Before long Alan and Cynthia's daughter Alison found herself working as a courier for Leger in Germany and Austria; youngest daughter Ailsa would work in the hotel contracting department.

Tragically, in June 1993, Alan Henry died suddenly at the age of just 54. Ian Henry, who had had joined the firm in 1989, now became Managing Director.

In December of 1993 investment company 3i Plc invested one million pounds in the company in exchange for 25 per cent of the business. By then Leger had already begun to sell its holidays through travel agents, including the major names such as Lunn Poly, Thomas Cook and Going Places: more expansion followed. In 1996 the company was appointed

Top left: Alan Henry founder of Leger Holidays. *Top right:* Leger Holidays brochures. *Left:* A Leger coach outside the Sunway House. *Below:* Two Leger drivers alongside one of the company's Silver Service coaches.

operators in the UK, offering holidays to every country in Europe - and beyond into Russia, America and India. The firm is also the largest operator of tours of the battlefields of Europe from the first and second world wars.

Throughout its existence Leger has been based in Rotherham. After a brief stay in Wickersely Leger has been located on Canklow Meadows Industrial Estate since 1989 where over 120 staff are now employed.

The small tour company founded by Alan Henry in his son's bedroom in 1982 now has an annual turnover of an incredible £30 million.

Yet for all its present size Leger remains committed to offering the same high standard of personal attention Alan Henry gave his customers all those years ago. Customers appreciate the Leger touch: one, a Mr Tomlinson from Burnley has been so impressed he has booked a church group holiday every

year since the Leger began, and in 2004 travelled for the 22nd time with 48 fellow travellers. Wonder if they still sing 'Ten Green Bottles'?

Top left, above left and bottom: *Views of the luxurious Leger Holidays Silver Service coaches.* ***Left:*** *Ian Henry, Managing Director of Leger Holidays.*

'preferred coach operator' to Disneyland Resort Paris, giving the business a major boost and generating an additional 80,000 customers a year.

Such a growth in the scale of operations inevitably brought Leger to the attention of larger firms. Airtours Plc (later named MyTravel Plc) bought the business in March 2000, though retaining Ian Henry as Managing Director. In 2002 however, the business was bought back from MyTravel in a management buy-out led by Ian Henry backed financially once again by 3i Plc.

Today there are some 50 coaches painted in the Leger livery, though Leger does not in fact own any coaches which are all operated by independent companies.

And what coaches they are. In 2003 Leger introduced its customers to 14 Silver Service coaches: now operating on many Leger tours the new vehicles feature extraordinary luxury. On Silver Service coaches there are only 36 seats installed instead of the usual 48; each coach features individual seat-back audio systems with headphones, and a leather seated lounge area at the rear of the vehicle.

From its small back bedroom start Leger is now one of the leading coach

Built to last

I f the building industry is not quite as old as the hills it can't be far behind them. Ever since man first realised what could be achieved by piling one stone on top of another he has been erecting structures ranging from the humblest hut to the mightiest of monuments.

But though builders and buildings have been with us for millennia building firms by contrast seem to come and go with depressing regularity. Happily however, there are notable exceptions which disprove that otherwise dismal rule.

Builders and contractors A Ryall & Son (Contractors) Limited, a company based in Victoria Road Mexborough, is today one of area's best known family owned businesses. Back in 1998 the firm was able to celebrate no less than half a century of corporate existence.

The company had a simple beginning in 1946 when the firms founder, the late Arthur Ryall, decided to leave his employer

Bramall & Ogden and set up in business with a work colleague Mr Webster. Ryall & Webster proved to be a short lived partnership which resulted in Arthur buying out his partner and founding his own firm on 18th June 1948; one of his first employees was his son Peter, hence the company name A Ryall & Son.

During the post war boom work was plentiful and the business was run from Tennyson Avenue in Mexborough, and a yard in Hampden Road. At the outset Arthur did most of the manual work and the quoting whilst son Peter trained as an apprentice bricklayer. The third generation of the Ryall family, Peter's son Nick, joined the company in 1979 after gaining an OND in Construction.

Top: Founder Arthur Ryall.
Above: Peter Ryall, son of Arthur.
Above right: Northcliffe Motors.
Right: An early project for A Ryall.
Below: A trip to JCB, Arthur Ryall can be seen extreme left and his wife Gertrud front third from left.

Until 1985 almost all of the company's work was for the National Coal Board, since then the need for other clients has spurred the firm to even more diversification. Today the company takes on work across the whole of Yorkshire and the East Midlands.

Locally however, many examples of Ryall's work can be seen: the Northcliffe Motors car showroom at Conisbrough, Mexborough's Adwick Road Créche and the new Grimethorpe Pentecostal Church.

Company founder Arthur Ryall passed away in 1989 at the age of 85; his son Peter passed away in 2001 leaving Nick Ryall to take the company forward into the 21st century.

The diversity of work now encompasses Airfields, Dock, Harbour and port settings, Leisure Centres, Schools and Colleges, Industrial and Retail Warehouses.

A Ryall & Son (Contractors) Limited now offers a comprehensive portfolio of construction work that includes design and build, alterations, conversions, fitting out, commissioning, renovation, repair, refurbishment, redecoration, decommissioning, demolition and dismantling. The company also carries out site preparation for any intended structure, including site clearance, exploration and investigation.

Today the original father & son team has grown to a workforce of 35. the company takes great pride in its staff many of whom have been trained in-house and has taken on at least one apprentice each year for many years, some of whom have subsequently left to start their own successful businesses. Many others have stayed.

Longest serving staff member is Fred Priestley, a lorry driver with four decades at 'Ryall's' under his belt; and at least three other employees who joined the company straight from school are hard on his heels having passed the 30 year mark as highlighted in the company's recent Investor in People recognition.

According to the company Mission Statement A Ryall & Son (Contractors) Limited strives to provide a building service beyond the expectations of all its customers. To maintain that level of service in an increasingly competitive market staff development and quality control are continually monitored and improved.

That kind of effort has paid dividends, with current annual turnover in excess of £3 million the company regularly wins contracts for work costing between £20,000 and £700,000 whilst still being happy to take on far smaller commissions on an individual basis.

As for the future, Nick Ryall has three sons of his own, at least one of whom will no doubt make a career in the firm founded by their Great Grandfather Arthur Ryall. Pending that day Nick Ryall continues to pursue the path of further expansion and diversification, building a business he intends to last for the generations yet to come.

Top left: *Goole Docks.*
Above left: *Gamston Airport.*
Right: *Stanley House.*
Below: *Nick Ryall with his sons Dominic, Thomas and Harry.*

Synonymous with quality and excellence since the 1870s

The Firm traces its roots back to William Gichard who founded the firm back in 1875 and who was, by all accounts, quite a character and a bon viveur. He was joined by his Nephew Stanley Gummer (who was sadly killed on the Somme in 1917). His Son-in-Law, Chris Furniss, then joined the Firm in 1918 having been a POW during the latter part of the Great War.

William Gichard died shortly thereafter and throughout the 1920s and 1930s Chris Furniss was a sole practitioner. During that time the mainstay of the business was Probate and Trust Work as well as Conveyancing. In 1936, he was joined by Sir Basil Rhodes and Harry Dunk as Articled Clerks

Again World events took centre stage and the practice ticked over during World War II. Sir Basil returned in 1946 (as a Lt Colonel in the York and Lancaster Regiment) as did Harry Dunk and both qualified in 1946. The Firm had its offices above the Midland Bank on College Street before moving

Below: Partner of Gichard & Co., Charles Rhodes (Senior Partner, seated) and Jeremy Copestake.

to its present premises on Doncaster Gate in 1960. Chris Furniss retired in 1965 thereby ending a family connection which had lasted some 90 years.

The connection continues to this day, however, through the Mason family (jewellers of great renown) who are still clients of the firm.

Sir Basil and Harry Dunk forged a very successful partnership during the 1960s and 1970s and expanded the work of the firm. It maintained its strong Will and Probate and Conveyancing practice as well as gaining an enhanced reputation for matrimonial work, litigation and licensing work. Both Sir Basil and Harry Dunk were well known characters in the area and would think nothing of turning up to defend a person for speeding, Sir Basil in his Aston Martin and Harry Dunk in his Jaguar! Michael Haywood joined the firm as a Junior Clerk in 1961 and John Barlow joined as a Junior Clerk in 1971. Both are still with the firm today as Legal Executives of great experience and reputation.

Sadly, Harry Dunk died in 1979. It was at this time that Christopher Middleton joined the Firm and became a Partner and later Judith Oliver (both whom later left to set up their own practice). Deborah Bates also joined as a Legal Executive in 1989.

Sir Basil's links with Rotherham are deep rooted indeed, having been born in the town and lived at Lane End House until the early 1960s. A Solicitor of prodigious talent, he managed to combine the law with a career in the Territorial Army (The Yorkshire Dragoons and Queens Own Yorkshire Yeomanry from 1946 until 1971), as well as a significant connection with Rotherham, becoming the Town's only Conservative Mayor in 1970/1971, High Sheriff of South Yorkshire in 1983 and a Deputy Lieutenant for South Yorkshire. He was the backbone of the Firm and sensing an opportunity during the early years of council house sales, acquired a branch office in Greasbrough.

The Family Firm feeling to the practice returned when Sir Basil's Son, Charles Rhodes, joined the practice as a Partner in 1991 having done his Articles at Wake Smith Solicitors in Sheffield. It was thanks to him that the Firm was the first in Rotherham to be awarded a Franchise by the Legal Aid Board in 1994 and the Firm still has a Specialist Quality Mark in the Family Category.

He has also masterminded the Firm's transition into modern technology and management methods which has significantly enhanced the way the firm carries out its business. After 57 years in practice, sadly Sir Basil Rhodes died in January 2003.

Charles Rhodes is now the Senior Partner and was joined in July 2003 as a Partner by an old friend, Jeremy Copestake, who was also an Articled Clerk at Wake Smith. Charles Rhodes specialises in Wills, Probate and Trust and Tax Planning and Jeremy Copestake specialises in Matrimonial work and Conveyancing (being a member of the Law Society Family Law Panel). Gichard & Co are blessed with 3 very experienced Legal Executives, Michael Haywood and John Barlow undertaking Conveyancing work and Deborah Bates undertaking matrimonial work. The Firm looks forward to the future having expanded further by taking on Samantha Woolley as a Trainee Solicitor (formerly a Barrister working at the Law Society). The Firm owes its success in no small measure to its very hard working, loyal and dedicated staff.

COUNTY BOROUGH OF ROTHERHAM
ELECTION OF COUNCILLORS 1971 —

PLEASE VOTE FOR

BASIL E. RHODES

THURSDAY, 13th MAY, 1971

SOUTH WARD

YOUR
CONSERVATIVE
CANDIDATE

Left: Sir Basil Rhodes as Conservative candidate for South Ward in 1971.

Acknowledgments

The publishers would like to thank

Rotherham MBC Archives & Local Studies Services

Mr Paul Fox at E Russum & Sons Ltd

FNT Lloyd-Jones

Roy Marshall

David Packer

W Ryan

Late SL Smith

Peter Thompson

Howard Turner

Andrew Mitchell

Steve Ainsworth

True North Books Ltd - Book List

Memories of Accrington - 1 903204 05 4

Memories of Barnet - 1 903204 16 X

Memories of Barnsley - 1 900463 11 3

Golden Years of Barnsley -1 900463 87 3

Memories of Basingstoke - 1 903204 26 7

Memories of Bedford - 1 900463 83 0

More Memories of Bedford - 1 903204 33 X

Golden Years of Birmingham - 1 900463 04 0

Birmingham Memories - 1 903204 45 3

Memories of Blackburn - 1 900463 40 7

More Memories of Blackburn - 1 900463 96 2

Memories of Blackpool - 1 900463 21 0

Memories of Bolton - 1 900463 45 8

More Memories of Bolton - 1 900463 13 X

Bolton Memories - 1 903204 37 2

Memories of Bournemouth -1 900463 44 X

Memories of Bradford - 1 900463 00 8

More Memories of Bradford - 1 900463 16 4

More Memories of Bradford II - 1 900463 63 6

Bradford Memories - 1 903204 47 X

Bradford City Memories - 1 900463 57 1

Memories of Bristol - 1 900463 78 4

More Memories of Bristol - 1 903204 43 7

Memories of Bromley - 1 903204 21 6

Memories of Burnley - 1 900463 95 4

Golden Years of Burnley - 1 900463 67 9

Memories of Bury - 1 900463 90 3

Memories of Cambridge - 1 900463 88 1

Memories of Cardiff - 1 900463 14 8

More Memories of Cardiff - 1 903204 73 9

Memories of Carlisle - 1 900463 38 5

Memories of Chelmsford - 1 903204 29 1

Memories of Cheltenham - 1 903204 17 8

Memories of Chester - 1 900463 46 6

More Memories of Chester -1 903204 02 X

Memories of Chesterfield -1 900463 61 X

More Memories of Chesterfield - 1 903204 28 3

Memories of Colchester - 1 900463 74 1

Nostalgic Coventry - 1 900463 58 X

Coventry Memories - 1 903204 38 0

Memories of Croydon - 1 900463 19 9

More Memories of Croydon - 1 903204 35 6

Golden Years of Darlington - 1 900463 72 5

Nostalgic Darlington - 1 900463 31 8

Darlington Memories - 1 903204 46 1

Memories of Derby - 1 900463 37 7

More Memories of Derby - 1 903204 20 8

Memories of Dewsbury & Batley - 1 900463 80 6

Memories of Doncaster - 1 900463 36 9

More Memories of Doncaster - 1 903204 75 5

Nostalgic Dudley - 1 900463 03 2

Golden Years of Dudley - 1 903204 60 7

Memories of Edinburgh - 1 900463 33 4

More memories of Edinburgh - 1903204 72 0

Memories of Enfield - 1 903204 14 3

Memories of Exeter - 1 900463 94 6

Memories of Glasgow - 1 900463 68 7

More Memories of Glasgow - 1 903204 44 5

Memories of Gloucester - 1 903204 04 6

Memories of Grimsby - 1 900463 97 0

More Memories of Grimsby - 1 903204 36 4

Memories of Guildford - 1 903204 22 4

Memories of Halifax - 1 900463 05 9

More Memories of Halifax - 1 900463 06 7

Golden Years of Halifax - 1 900463 62 8

Nostalgic Halifax - 1 903204 30 5

Memories of Harrogate - 1 903204 01 1

Memories of Hartlepool - 1 900463 42 3

Memories of High Wycombe - 1 900463 84 9

Memories of Huddersfield - 1 900463 15 6

More Memories of Huddersfield - 1 900463 26 1

Golden Years of Huddersfield - 1 900463 77 6

Nostalgic Huddersfield - 1 903204 19 4

Huddersfield Town FC - 1 900463 51 2

Memories of Hull - 1 900463 86 5

More Memories of Hull - 1 903204 06 2

Hull Memories - 1 903204 70 4

Memories of Ipswich - 1 900463 09 1

More Memories of Ipswich - 1 903204 52 6

Memories of Keighley - 1 900463 01 6

Golden Years of Keighley - 1 900463 92 X

True North Books Ltd - Book List

Memories of Kingston - 1 903204 24 0

Memories of Leeds - 1 900463 75 X

More Memories of Leeds - 1 900463 12 1

Golden Years of Leeds - 1 903204 07 0

Memories of Leicester - 1 900463 08 3

Leeds Memories - 1 903204 62 3

More Memories of Leicester - 1 903204 08 9

Memories of Leigh - 1 903204 27 5

Memories of Lincoln - 1 900463 43 1

Memories of Liverpool - 1 900463 07 5

More Memories of Liverpool - 1 903204 09 7

Liverpool Memories - 1 903204 53 4

Memories of Luton - 1 900463 93 8

Memories of Macclesfield - 1 900463 28 8

Memories of Manchester - 1 900463 27 X

More Memories of Manchester - 1 903204 03 8

Manchester Memories - 1 903204 54 2

Memories of Middlesbrough - 1 900463 56 3

More Memories of Middlesbrough - 1 903204 42 9

Memories of Newbury - 1 900463 79 2

Memories of Newcastle - 1 900463 81 4

More Memories of Newcastle - 1 903204 10 0

Newcastle Memories - 1.903204 71 2

Memories of Newport - 1 900463 59 8

Memories of Northampton - 1 900463 48 2

More Memories of Northampton - 1 903204 34 8

Memories of Norwich - 1 900463 73 3

Memories of Nottingham - 1 900463 91 1

More Memories of Nottingham - 1 903204 11 9

Nottingham Memories - 1 903204 63 1

Bygone Oldham - 1 900463 25 3

Memories of Oldham - 1 900463 76 8

Memories of Oxford - 1 900463 54 7

Memories of Peterborough - 1 900463 98 9

Golden Years of Poole - 1 900463 69 5

Memories of Portsmouth - 1 900463 39 3

More Memories of Portsmouth - 1 903204 51 8

Nostalgic Preston - 1 900463 50 4

More Memories of Preston - 1 900463 17 2

Preston Memories - 1 903204 41 0

Memories of Reading - 1 900463 49 0

Memories of Rochdale - 1 900463 60 1

More Memories of Reading - 1 903204 39 9

More Memories of Rochdale - 1 900463 22 9

Memories of Romford - 1 903204 40 2

Memories of Rotherham - 1 903204 77 1

Memories of St Albans - 1 903204 23 2

Memories of St Helens - 1 900463 52 0

Memories of Sheffield - 1 900463 20 2

More Memories of Sheffield - 1 900463 32 6

Golden Years of Sheffield - 1 903204 13 5

Memories of Slough - 1 900 463 29 6

Golden Years of Solihull - 1 903204 55 0

Memories of Southampton - 1 900463 34 2

More Memories of Southampton - 1 903204 49 6

Memories of Stockport - 1 900463 55 5

More Memories of Stockport - 1 903204 18 6

Memories of Stockton - 1 900463 41 5

Memories of Stoke-on-Trent - 1 900463 47 4

More Memories of Stoke-on-Trent - 1 903204 12 7

Memories of Stourbridge - 1903204 31 3

Memories of Sunderland - 1 900463 71 7

More Memories of Sunderland - 1 903204 48 8

Memories of Swindon - 1 903204 00 3

Memories of Uxbridge - 1 900463 64 4

Memories of Wakefield - 1 900463 65 2

More Memories of Wakefield - 1 900463 89 X

Nostalgic Walsall - 1 900463 18 0

Golden Years of Walsall - 1 903204 56 9

More Memories of Warrington - 1 900463 02 4

Memories of Watford - 1 900463 24 5

Golden Years of West Bromwich - 1 900463 99 7

Memories of Wigan - 1 900463 85 7

Golden Years of Wigan - 1 900463 82 2

Nostalgic Wirral - 1 903204 15 1

Wirral Memories - 1 903204 747

Memories of Woking - 1 903204 32 1

Nostalgic Wolverhampton - 1 900463 53 9

Wolverhampton Memories - 1 903204 50 X

Memories of Worcester - 1 903204 25 9

Memories of Wrexham - 1 900463 23 7

Memories of York - 1 900463 66 0